Cambridge Poetry Workshop
GCSE

CAMBRIDGE POETRY WORKSHOP GCSE

Jeffrey and Lynn Wood

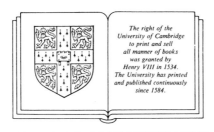

The right of the
University of Cambridge
to print and sell
all manner of books
was granted by
Henry VIII in 1534.
The University has printed
and published continuously
since 1584.

CAMBRIDGE UNIVERSITY PRESS

Cambridge

New York   New Rochelle

Melbourne   Sydney

To our parents

Authors' acknowledgements

The encouragement, suggestions and constructive criticism of many
colleagues and the responses of our students to these units as they were
being written has helped make this book what it is. We wish particularly to
thank Jill Rendell for her unflagging service at the wordprocessor, and
Keith Rose of CUP and Katherine James for their painstaking attention to
detail as well as for numerous wise suggestions about where this sentence
could be less opaque, that assignment more lively. The shortcomings which
remain are ours alone.

Published by the Press Syndicate of the University of Cambridge
The Pitt Building, Trumpington Street, Cambridge CB2 1RP
32 East 57th Street, New York, NY 10022, USA
10 Stamford Road, Oakleigh, Melbourne 3166, Australia

© Cambridge University Press 1988

First published 1988
Reprinted 1988

Printed in Great Britain by Scotprint, Musselburgh, Scotland

British Library cataloguing in publication data

Wood, Jeffrey
Cambridge poetry workshop GCSE.
I. Title   II. Wood, Lynn
821'.0076

ISBN 0 521 33672 4 paperback

GO

CONTENTS

v

POETS

William Shakespeare	1564–1616
John Donne	1572–1631
Andrew Marvell	1621–1678
John Scott of Amwell	1730–1783
John Keats	1795–1821
Alfred, Lord Tennyson	1809–1892
Robert Browning	1812–1889
Thomas Hardy	1840–1928
Walter de la Mare	1873–1956
Robert Frost	1874–1963
Carl Sandburg	1878–1967
D.H. Lawrence	1885–1930
Rupert Brooke	1887–1915
Edwin Muir	1887–1959
T.S. Eliot	1888–1965
Wilfred Owen	1893–1918
W.H. Auden	1907–1973
Dylan Thomas	1914–1953
D.J. Enright	1920–
Edwin Morgan	1920–
Vernon Scannell	1922–
Anthony Hecht	1923–
Miroslav Holub	1923–
Louis Simpson	1923–
John Wain	1925–
Thom Gunn	1929–
Ted Hughes	1930–
Adrian Henri	1932–
Sylvia Plath	1932–1963
Yevgeny Yevtushenko	1933–
Roger McGough	1937–
Seamus Heaney	1939–
Eileen McAuley	1969–

To the teacher

In *Cambridge Poetry Workshop* we have set out to provide a significant classroom resource: a substantial number of self-contained teaching units, each of which presents a major poem (or pair of poems) and then leads, through individual or group explorations of the poem's themes and language, to a variety of creative and critical activities accessible to the full range of students. The units in the present volume include specific assignments for both GCSE English and GCSE English Literature.

The units may be used as they stand but they are not intended to be 'teacher-proof'. Many ways will suggest themselves to you in which units may be adapted, modified and extended, and many of the strategies we suggest for particular poems will be equally successful with others. What we hope will be useful is a strong framework with a variety of tried and tested assignments. All of the material in this book has been used successfully with students in very different schools and in a variety of teaching situations.

Most of the units are appropriate for individual and small group study but they can also be used for whole class work, the teacher using the questions to initiate and develop discussion, as starting points for exploring both the text and the experience the poem dramatises. Certain units (identified by asterisks on the Contents page) may be used to develop students' confidence in 'unseen' criticism and offer a useful way of gauging how confident individuals and groups are becoming in exploring texts for themselves.

Strategy

As a rule, each unit consists of the following: a preamble, mapping the themes and/or emotional territory of the poem; the text (with full glossary); a number of Thinking/Talking Points which encourage close study of the poem; and a choice of creative and critical Assignments. The teacher decides approximately how much time a particular group of students may be expected to take over each stage. The unit on poems by Yevtushenko and Sandburg (pages 195–97), for example, might be organised as three one-hour lesson units: an hour's preparatory work where students discuss varieties of lying, perhaps recalling their own experiences or hunting through a pile of newspapers and magazines for examples and then writing something to illustrate a particular kind of lying; an hour's close work on the two texts relating them to the previous lesson's research; and then a one-hour session of critical and/or creative work arising. But the whole unit would also work as a single lesson activity.

English teaching is often most exciting when it is most opportunist, free to respond to the direction a discussion or assignment takes. Wherever possible, it is best to allow group work to develop at its own pace and in its own directions. Some of the most interesting creative 'responses' we have had to Keats's *Nightingale* (page 135), for example, were produced after the preamble session, *before* the class had read the poem. It was striking how many 'Keatsian' details – not only of mood and sentiment but even of texture and rhythm – the students' own pieces contained. If our experience is typical, as students become more confident about exploring their own experiences and concerns, the preambles will often develop a life of their own, seemingly independent of the poem to which they lead. After such creative explorations, and having studied and talked about the poem, critical work often shows an attention to and understanding of subtle points of poetic technique which is much more confident, searching and lively than a conventional lit. crit. approach would have produced.

But, equally often, it can be helpful to have a framework to fall back upon, a structure of leading questions to work through which rescue discussion from circularity, and a range of clearly structured activities with sufficient variety and choice to appeal to a wide cross-section of students. It is not always easy to invent such activities on the hoof and while we hope we have avoided a prescriptive approach to the study of poetry, we have certainly tried to avoid vagueness. 'Write about the poem in any way you like' is not a very helpful instruction to students who have limited literary experience.

Preliminaries

If one characteristic of poetry is intensity – language charged with meaning in the exploration of powerful human experiences – then that very intensity is something a listener/reader needs to be prepared for. It is disconcerting to enter a room to find somebody in a rapture of grief or perplexity or delight. There are many reasons why adolescents register discomfort about poetry. Surely one of them is simply embarrassment and confusion on encountering an inexplicable outpouring of joy or desolation. We feel 'the emotional territory' of a poem usually needs to be mapped in advance. If the situation is emotionally (and thereafter, intellectually) comprehensible to students, it will be because it echoes, touches upon some sympathetic chord in their own histories, reflections, fantasies, hopes and fears. Often we ask questions to which the answers are best left confidential: 'Jot down some of the feelings you think you might have in such a situation . . . See if you can draw a picture or a diagram of how you felt last time somebody behaved like that towards you . . .'. It is a mistake to demand that intimate and intense areas of concern are all shared publicly, even in a small group. Although, as George Eliot observed, silence does not always brood over a full nest, a quiet class is not necessarily a disengaged one. Poetry plays a valuable part in the education of feeling – giving young people a vocabulary with which to explore and discuss things which deeply concern them and which may be aired nowhere else. For this reason, a variety of teaching contexts – individual, small group and plenary discussion – is particularly appropriate. If we want to help students own and articulate their perceptions of the world, we must encourage them to talk about what most concerns them but we must also respect their right to some privacy.

On the other hand, we do not advocate mapping in advance 'the verbal territory' of a poem. To present a class with a list of hard words that they are about to encounter (probably used in exacting ways) and to drill them in definitions before they are aware of the context, or have any particular desire to acquire such arcane knowledge, seems guaranteed to kill any kind of spontaneous engagement with language, let alone with the situation the poem explores. Eliot observed that 'It is a test . . . that genuine poetry can communicate before it is understood'. To see a poem as a verbal hurdle for which a bit of linguistic (or worse still, lit. crit.) limbering-up is the necessary preliminary, is to see poetry as an object, an end in itself, rather than as an expressive means to an end.

Preliminaries: reading aloud

What Hopkins said about his own verse, is true of most of the poetry in this volume: '. . . you must not slovenly read it with the eyes but with your ears, as if the paper were declaiming it at you'. Most poetry is written to be heard; it comes to life in performance. There was no obvious way of producing the *Workshop* so that it was physically impossible to turn to the Thinking/Talking Points before the poem had been read aloud (and then read and reread!), but we would urge that, wherever possible, the poems are read to the class, more than once if possible, *before* the students look at the poems as marks on a page. Once the text becomes the focus of discussion, it is essential to pause now and again to allow the students to read the poem to themselves at their own pace, and from time to time for them again to hear the whole poem read aloud: if you can persuade them to close their eyes while you do that, the benefits will be considerable.

The glossaries

If the most important thing an English teacher does in the classroom is to read aloud, lifting words off the page, we feel the textbook's most important function is to make the surface of the language accessible.

It is curious that although few editions of Shakespeare lack extensive glossaries, prose and poetry equally remote from the language experience of most of our students is usually presented to them bald and intractable. In our experience, a large part of the anxiety/hostility which poetry sometimes produces in readers is no more than confusion and irritation: somebody is playing a game and refusing to divulge the rules. How does any of us feel, confronted by a page of unfamiliar words? Poetry often seems to turn up wrapped in a code – alien, glass-cased – and gets rejected, like the boy in the playground who refuses to talk in a language anybody can understand. And we are surely not the only teachers guilty of lapsing into the game, 'I know the meaning of a long word you don't know . . .' and believing that that was teaching literature? If poetry is misused in this way, to keep students in their place, it is little wonder that it sometimes engenders hostility.

The glossary is a way of giving poetry away; and of making the business of looking it up (part of enjoying most poetry) as effortless and as speedy as possible. It is so boring for everyone in the group to have to trudge through every word that anyone doesn't know: 'Hands up who knows the meaning of "colloped".' (see *Childe Roland*). And the small dictionaries usually available to students are little help when it comes to the precise shades of meaning exploited in a poem.

Of course, glossing is a notoriously perilous business. Wishing to 'give poetry away' is easier than doing it. We have tried to be consistent, attempting always to gloss an unfamiliar with a more familiar word or phrase, even at the cost of exactness. Thus the glossed definitions are sometimes no more than starting-points for close verbal scrutiny where you may feel that it is appropriate for a particular group. Our concern has been to guide students into the situation of the poem as quickly as possible. Although poets do sometimes erect barriers to delay explorers, we believe that most would be sorry if students found them characteristically unintelligible.

We should be grateful to receive your comments both on the general principle of glossing and on particular examples which you feel are simply wrong or could be better done.

The Thinking/Talking Points

These are intended to be just that – sometimes to encourage a student's private mulling over of a poem's impact on her/him, sometimes to prompt large or small group discussion. They are not intended and will not work as comprehension exercises. If we have asked a large number of questions it is not in some factitious quest for final answers.

Yet we have chosen poems here which use language in a masterly way; part of the enjoyment of them is relishing the peculiar aptness of this phrase, the deliberate ambiguity of that one. To skim a great poem, to read it merely as a bit of clumsily executed prose, a passing illustration of some general theme, is to miss its particular, exciting, exacting richness; there are certain matters of syntax and basic prose sense which we feel need identifying. But on the whole few of our questions will yield answers to be marked right or wrong. Most of them are designed to signpost, to provoke, not to predetermine responses. The good questions will breed further questions from the students.

Working with a whole class, we find it is usually best to give the students some time to do their own thinking and jotting around the Thinking/Talking Points before bringing everyone together to talk. Where feelings, judgements and values are being examined, we should not demand answers to pop out like solutions to maths problems. Forcing the pace is the most common shortcoming in student-teachers working on verse. From time to time, it is a handy corrective to study one's own processes in coming to terms with the demanding and unfamiliar – perhaps something like a Pound Canto or one of Browning's extended pieces – to remind oneself of what the experience of meeting an unfamiliar poem is like. The last thing one wants, five minutes after being given a strange text, is to have all sorts of complicated questions fired at one: 'Can you think of seven different meanings for "etiolated" in line 42?'. The vague questions are worse than the specific ones: 'Do you like the poem?' If a poem is worth doing, we have to allow it time to unfold itself.

Our job as teachers is to respond to our students' responses; to listen to the stage they have reached and to take care neither to underestimate what the circuits can cope with nor to overload them. Nor to impose an 'adult' reading over one more congruent to the student's own experience of things. It is difficult to strike the proper balance between a pedantic, prescriptive 'reading' of a text and one which is impressionistic, superficial, perhaps foolish. A poem is a meeting-place; unlike chapters in textbooks, poems continuously grow with their readers. None of us reads the same *Macbeth* at sixteen and at sixty. We know when a poem is a great one when it means a bit more rather than a bit less each time we read it.

Most of our questions, therefore, unlike comprehension questions, are bound to receive different, provisional answers from different students at different stages in their life and language awareness, emotional and intellectual development. It is unnecessary to force the pace. The poem will still be there in a year's time when the student has developed, both as a person and as a reader. The teacher will have grown too. It is very easy, especially when a poem is a particular favourite, to fall into the trap of trying to 'exhaust' it in a couple of lessons which quickly degenerate from collective exploration into one-person expositions: 'What the poet is saying here is . . .'. All that we are likely to exhaust by doing that is our students! In the end, poems are their own best advocates. Once the territory has been opened up, they go on working long after the lesson has been forgotten.

Such teaching requires considerable disinterestedness. It is such a long way from what too many of us experienced in the sixth form or at college where 'Guess the answer in my head' or 'Look it up in *A Reader's Guide*' was too often the name of the lit. crit. game. A poem does not exist independently of a reader: its meaning is a collaboration of text and personal response.

The Assignments

In GCSE English and English Literature courses where a substantial proportion, if not all, of the marks are for coursework, one of the problems most frequently encountered in the classroom is simply that of organising students' folders, particularly towards the end of the course.

We have made a distinction between what are primarily creative, personal responses to poems (English Assignments) and those in which attention to the text of the poem is central (English Literature Assignments). In practice, these distinctions may sometimes be blurred and you may want to adjust an English Assignment slightly so that it can qualify as an English Literature one (particularly as 'evidence of wider reading') or as a response to reading a complete work of literature for the English file. It seemed preferable for us to over-organise assignments than to run the risk of the end of every session resounding to the chorus: 'Is this a bit of English work or English Literature?'

We have not attempted to differentiate tasks in some putative order of difficulty. English is one of the few subjects where it is possible to frame a question (e.g. Why did Macbeth kill Duncan?) to which there is a genuinely full spectrum of possible answers. Designing a dust-jacket or writing a diary-entry can certainly involve as high a level of critical interrogation as producing a traditional essay – and be much more interesting to assess! Nevertheless, you will probably wish to intervene at times to influence or limit students' choices: 'I think it's time you did an assignment where . . .' to ensure that a variety of types of writing and other creative work is tackled during the course.

A note on 'assinence and illiteration'

There can be few more depressing experiences than reading A-level unseens which begin: 'The poem has a rhyme scheme ababbadaea' . . . [it doesn't] 'and is written in writhing cutlets in antiseptic metre . . . In line 6 is some illiteration and two words which use assinence: "brown" and "egg-box". The poet uses the image of the girl as a cymbal of suffering . . .' [he doesn't].

Technical terms may have their uses with some academic classes with certain very experienced teachers, but we believe that the dangers of using them far outweigh their utility. For too many students, tracking down a bit of technique becomes not merely a distraction from the theme of the poem but an end in itself; not just an escape from, but a block to responding, to seeing the poem at all. Technical terminology is frequently misunderstood, and as an aesthetic tool, we believe a technical term is a poor substitute for the student's own language: 'I like the brutal sounds of the harsh words *bent-double . . . beggars under sacks . . . cursing like hags . . .* piled on top of one another. They help you to feel the disgust, the squalor, the ugliness of it all . . .'

Intellectualising, something which many English graduates have been forced to do to show that an English degree is as real as one in Physics, is something they must unlearn quickly if they are to take poetry into the classroom. Sharing a poem means, above all, exploring an intense human experience, with all the uncertainties and dangerous potential which life has. It does call for openness, for a genuine provisionality, a degree of surrender on the part of the teacher: there are no safe, right answers; there will be some challenges which it will not be easy to dismiss. When we feel vulnerable, we fall back on intellectual gymnastics and exclusive terminology. We hope those who have felt uncomfortable talking about poetry as human experience will find the *Workshop* gives them a structure with which to develop techniques and gain confidence. Once poetry starts to spark in the classroom, nothing can be more exciting.

Jeffrey and Lynn Wood
Cambridge, 1988

Shakespeare
from AS YOU
LIKE IT

Baby . . . toddler . . . pupil . . . teenager . . . newly-wed . . . parent . . .

What would be your own list of the parts a person plays during his/her lifetime? (Think about the different roles you have played already. What roles do you suppose await you over the next sixty years or so?)

Decide upon the six, seven or eight stages which more or less everyone passes through. See if you can find a couple of phrases to describe behaviour which belongs to each particular phase and to no other (e.g. baby: crawling into mischief, howling for its bottle . . .; teenager: sneaking behind the bikesheds, telling Dad where he's got it wrong . . .).

If we do all play a number of different *parts* in our lifetime, are we all performers in a play? (Does getting through life successfully entail being a versatile actor? Who writes the script? Who directs? What does the audience hope to see?)

The following lines come from a play written by an actor. Perhaps because he was used to seeing the same people playing lots of different parts, Shakespeare was struck by the extent to which all life is like a performance, people changing roles and always – to some extent – acting.

Read through the extract three or four times before considering the points which follow.

The Seven Ages

All the world's a stage,
And all the men and women merely players;
They have their exits and their entrances,
And one man in his time plays many parts,
His acts being seven ages.   *5*
        At first the infant,
Mewling and puking in the nurse's arms: ***mewling*** *crying like a cat.*
Then the whining schoolboy, with his satchel
And shining morning face, creeping like snail
Unwillingly to school.   *10*
        And then the lover,
Sighing like furnace, with a woeful ballad   ***woeful ballad*** *sad, sorry*
Made to his mistress' eyebrow.   *song.*

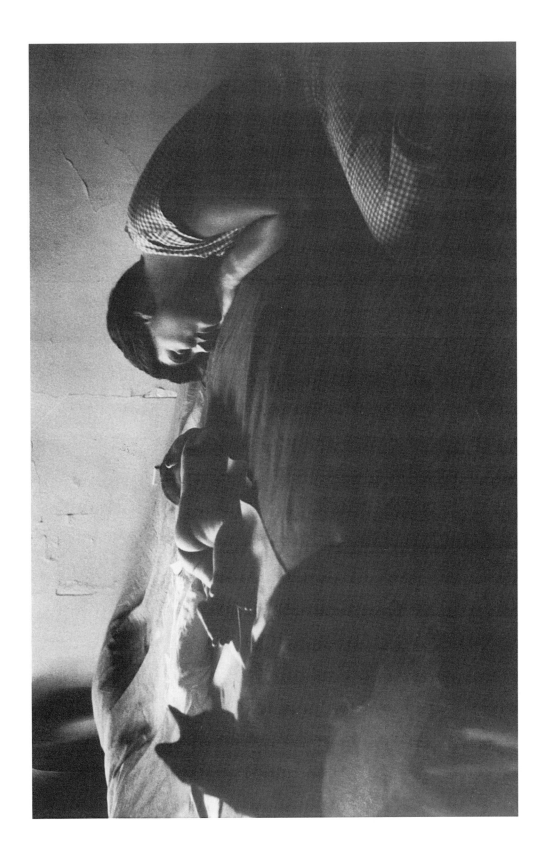

                         Then, a soldier,
Full of strange oaths, and bearded like the pard,   15   **pard** *leopard.*
Jealous in honour, sudden and quick in quarrel,   **jealous in honour** *touchy*
Seeking the bubble reputation   *if he thinks his honour is in*
Even in the cannon's mouth.   *question.*
                         And then, the justice,   **justice** *magistrate.*
In fair round belly, with good capon lin'd   20   **with good capon lin'd**
With eyes severe and beard of formal cut,   *having fed on a good capon*
Full of wise saws, and modern instances,   *(perhaps a bribe).*
And so he plays his part.   **wise saws** *sensible sayings.*
                         The sixth age shifts
Into the lean and slipper'd pantaloon,   25
With spectacles on nose, and pouch on side,
His youthful hose well sav'd, a world too wide   **hose** *breeches.*
For his shrunk shank; and his big manly voice,   **shank** *leg from knee to*
Turning again toward childish treble, pipes   *ankle.*
And whistles in his sound.   30
                         Last scene of all,
That ends this strange eventful history,
Is second childishness and mere oblivion;
Sans teeth, sans eyes, sans taste, sans everything.   **sans** *without.*

                    from *As You Like It* Act II sc. vii

Thinking/Talking Points

▷   Did any of Shakespeare's 'seven ages' correspond with the ones you decided
     upon? Which of his pictures of man's seven ages do you find most effective?

▷   What do you think the speaker is implying about the lover who writes, 'to his
     mistress' *eyebrow*'?

▷   Why do you think the speaker refers to the fame a soldier seeks as a 'bubble'?

▷   Why do you think the *first* detail we are given about the magistrate is 'In fair
     round belly . . .'? What is being implied about him?

▷   How does the speaker capture the sound of an old man's voice?

▷   Suggest two or three extra phrases to describe each of the ages in this list.

Reread the extract and then choose an assignment.

Assignments

English

○ *The Seven Ages: The Revised Version.*
Write your own version of this speech, in verse or prose, adapted to modern times.

○ *My Favourite Role(s).*
Write about one or two of the parts you have had to play so far in your life. Do you look back nostalgically to any particular role you played (e.g. as a toddler or as a Brownie or as the captain of a school team)?
See if you can recapture some of the feelings you had then.
You may like to illustrate your piece with some old photographs of yourself.

○ *Scenes from a Life.*
(This is an activity which could be shared amongst a group of you with each person responsible for one age.) Imagine you are making a long-term documentary about a person's life, with interviews every ten years or so and a review of what has happened to your subject since the previous programme.
Begin by sketching out the biographical details of your subject (e.g. date and place of birth; family; school career; first job; marriage; etc.) and then decide on the dates of your five/six programmes about him/her.
Give each programme the same overall shape but try to avoid making your subject's progress too predictable.

○ When a famous person dies, newspapers sometimes print an *obituary* of him/her – an account of the person's life and an assessment of his/her career. Write an imaginary obituary of yourself, recording the landmarks in your career: (e.g. After a brilliant three years at Oxford when she was the first student to receive, simultaneously, first-class degrees in Divinity, Physics and Gymnastics, she pursued a dual career as actress and astronaut, giving the first performance of *Hedda Gabler* on Mars in 1997 . . .)

Background material

Granada Television: World in Action   *Seven Up*

★

YOU'RE

Here's a poem which is a riddle.
See if you can figure it out.

You're

Clownlike, happiest on your hands,
Feet to the stars, and moon-skulled,
Gilled like a fish. A common-sense
Thumbs-down on the dodo's mode.
Wrapped up in yourself like a spool,   5
Trawling your dark as owls do.
Mute as a turnip from the Fourth
Of July to All Fools' Day,
O high-riser, my little loaf.

Vague as fog and looked for like mail.   10
Farther off than Australia.
Bent-backed Atlas, our traveled prawn.
Snug as a bud and at home
Like a sprat in a pickle jug.
A creel of eels, all ripples.   15
Jumpy as a Mexican bean.
Right, like well-done sum.
A clean slate, with your own face on.

dodo *an extinct bird, larger than a turkey, which had useless wings.*
mode *way of life.*
trawling *(literally) fishing, pulling a net along the sea-bottom.*
mute *silent, unspeaking.*

Atlas *a mythological giant who held up the sky.*

sprat *tiny sea fish.*
creel *fisherman's wicker basket.*

When you have spent some time puzzling your way through the poem,
consider the following points.

Thinking/Talking Points

▷   How many kinds of behaviour can you think of which are 'clownlike'?

▷   Roughly how long is it from the Fourth of July to All Fools' Day?
What do you associate with each date?
Why will the subject of the poem cease to be 'mute' on All Fools' day?

▷   Why does the subject of the poem give the 'dodo's mode' the 'thumbs-down'?

▷   How do you think a sprat would behave if you put it into a pickle jug?
Or an eel in a creel?

▷ How do owls hunt?

▷ If you called someone a 'little loaf' and a 'high-riser'
  (a) what would the two ideas have in common?
  (b) what other, independent meanings might the phrases have?

▷ How do you feel as you wait for a letter to arrive?

▷ If you are in Britain, how can someone who is so close to you that you can feel him/her jumping be 'Farther off than Australia'?

▷ When is someone's face like 'A clean slate'?

▷ 'To the stars' is a phrase often used as part of a school's motto.
  What does the phrase suggest about a person's potential?

▷ In what sense(s) can a person be 'wrapped up' in themselves 'like a spool'?

▷ Can you think of other senses in which the subject of this poem resembles a turnip, other than by being silent?

▷ Why are there so many fishy images in this poem?

▷ What pictures and feelings does the phrase 'moon-skulled' suggest to you?

▷ How can 'a bud' be like a 'traveled prawn'? Or like Atlas?

▷ Why (exactly) is the subject of this poem like a 'sum'?
  Can you write out the sum?
  How does the speaker know the sum was *right*?

When you think you have solved the riddle, suggest some phrases of your own to describe the subject of this poem in riddle-fashion.

(If you're still stuck for the answer to the riddle, see page 164.)

Assignments

English

○ Write a riddle-poem of your own about something or someone. Here are a few suggestions: a pet; Mum or Dad; a motorway; a newspaper; sports day; a game of cards; a toddler.

English Literature

○ Essay: How successfully has Sylvia Plath shared her feelings about the subject of this poem? Which details did you find most/least convincing?

Further reading

Plath   *Metaphors* (in *The Colossus*)
        Morning Song (in *Ariel*)

★

de la Mare
DRY AUGUST BURNED

Heaney
THE EARLY PURGES

Read through the following poems carefully two or three times; think about what they have in common.

Dry August Burned

Dry August burned. A harvest hare
Limp on the kitchen table lay,
Its fur blood-blubbered, eyes astare,
While a small child that stood near by
Wept out her heart to see it there.   5

Sharp came the *clop* of hoofs, the clang
Of dangling chain, voices that rang.
Out like a leveret she ran,   *leveret a young hare.*
To feast her glistening bird-clear eyes
On a team of field-artillery,   10
Gay, to manoeuvres, thudding by.   *manoeuvres military*
Spur and gun and limber plate   *exercises.*
Flashed in the sun. Alert, elate,   *limber plate part of a gun-*
Noble horses, foam at lip,   *carriage.*
                                                                elate in high spirits.
Harness, stirrup, holster, whip,   15
She watched the sun-tanned soldiery
Till dust-white hedge had hidden away –
Its din into rumour thinned –
The laughing, jolting, wild array;
And then – the wonder and tumult gone –   20
Stood nibbling a green leaf, alone,
Her dark eyes, dreaming . . . She turned, and ran,
Elf-like, into the house again.
The hare had vanished . . . 'Mother,' she said,
Her tear-stained cheek now flushed with red,   25
'Please, may I go and see it skinned?'

☆

The Early Purges

I was six when I first saw kittens drown.
Dan Taggart pitched them, 'the scraggy wee shits',
Into a bucket; a frail metal sound,

purges getting rid of undesirables.

Soft paws scraping like mad. But their tiny din
Was soon soused. They were slung on the snout   5
Of the pump and the water pumped in.

soused quenched.

'Sure isn't it better for them now?' Dan said.
Like wet gloves they bobbed and shone till he sluiced
Them out on the dunghill, glossy and dead.

sluiced flushed.

Suddenly frightened, for days I sadly hung   10
Round the yard, watching the three sogged remains
Turn mealy and crisp as old summer dung

mealy pale.

Until I forgot them. But the fear came back
When Dan trapped big rats, snared rabbits, shot crows
Or, with a sickening tug, pulled old hens' necks.   15

Still, living displaces false sentiments
And now, when shrill pups are prodded to drown
I just shrug, 'Bloody pups'. It makes sense:

displaces false sentiments gets rid of phoney feelings.

'Prevention of cruelty' talk cuts ice in town
Where they consider death unnatural   20
But on well-run farms pests have to be kept down.

Thinking/Talking Points

Dry August Burned

▷ How would you describe the child's attitude to the hare at the beginning of the poem?
What questions, reflections, feelings do you imagine running through her head?

▷ What is the child's attitude to the hare at the end of the poem?
How does the poet remind us of how she felt earlier?
Can you explain what has happened to alter her outlook?

▷ Look again at lines 6−20.
What impression do those lines give you of the soldiers?
What feelings do those lines prompt?
What do you think the poet's attitude to soldiers was?

▷ 'Stood nibbling a green leaf, alone'
What do you think might be passing through the girl's mind at this point?
What is ironic about describing her in this way?

Reread the poem and then look again at *The Early Purges*.

The Early Purges

▷   What similarities do you notice between the situation in this poem and the one in *Dry August Burned*?
     Do you think the poet's attitude to the change in the child is similar?

▷   What connection does the poem imply between violent language and violent behaviour?
     How would you describe the difference beween the words 'kittens' (line 1) and 'pests' (line 21). What pictures do the two words suggest to you?

▷   What is your impression of Dan Taggart? (How do you picture him? Can you imagine the way he walks?)
     Why do you think the boy is impressed by him?

▷   What do you notice about the changes in the way the speaker describes the kittens?
     'frail . . . Soft paws . . . tiny . . . Like wet gloves . . .'
     'glossy and dead . . . sogged . . . mealy and crisp as old summer dung . . .'
     Do you think that last description was the sort which the boy would have used before he met Dan?

▷   '. . . living displaces false sentiments'
     Do you agree with the speaker's assessment of what has happened?

     Look carefully at the two poems again before choosing an assignment.

Assignments

English

○   Describe an experience which changed your attitude to human or animal suffering in some way. Do you feel that the way a person treats animals tells us anything about how she/he feels about human beings?

○   Essay: To what extent do you agree with the sentiments expressed here:
     '"Prevention of cruelty" talk cuts ice in town
     Where they consider death unnatural,
     But on well-run farms pests have to be kept down.'?
     Do you think efficiency is more important than anything else, even if it results in suffering?
     Discuss particular cases where you feel attitudes to animals need to be examined carefully. (e.g. You may wish to discuss factory farming; vivisection; the training of animals for sport; the breeding of animals for exhibition.)

English Literature

○   Essay: With close reference to the texts of the two poems, compare and contrast the way the outlook of each child was changed.
     In what sense(s) have the children 'lost their innocence'?

★

OUT, OUT –

In Shakespeare's *Othello*, the hero, destroyed by jealousy, comes to his sleeping wife's bed to murder her. As he looks from her to the candle which lights the room, he reflects upon how fragile human life is:

> 'Put out the light, and then put out the light;
> If I quench thee, thou flaming minister,
> I can again thy former light restore,
> Should I repent me; but once put out thine,
> Thou cunning'st pattern of excelling nature,
> I know not where is that Promethean heat
> That can thy light relume . . .'

A similar image haunts Macbeth's weary final moments as he contemplates his own inevitable extinction:

>   'Out, out, brief candle!
> Life's but a walking shadow; a poor player
> That struts and frets his hour upon the stage,
> And then is heard no more; it is a tale
> Told by an idiot, full of sound and fury,
> Signifying nothing.'

Read through the following poem carefully two or three times before looking at the points which follow.

Out, Out –

The buzz saw snarled and rattled in the yard	
And made dust and dropped stove-length sticks of wood,	
Sweet-scented stuff when the breeze drew across it.	
And from there those that lifted eyes could count	
Five mountain ranges one behind the other	5
Under the sunset far into Vermont.	
And the saw snarled and rattled, snarled and rattled,	
As it ran light, or had to bear a load.	
And nothing happened: day was all but done.	
Call it a day, I wish they might have said	10
To please the boy by giving him the half hour	
That a boy counts so much when saved from work.	
His sister stood beside them in her apron	
To tell them 'Supper'. At the word, the saw,	
As if to prove saws knew what supper meant,	15
Leaped out at the boy's hand, or seemed to leap –	
He must have given the hand. However it was,	
Neither refused the meeting. But the hand!	
The boy's first outcry was a rueful laugh,	

Vermont *a rural state in New England (USA).*

rueful *regretful.*

As he swung toward them holding up the hand   *20*
Half in appeal, but half as if to keep
The life from spilling. Then the boy saw all –
Since he was old enough to know, big boy
Doing a man's work, though a child at heart –
He saw all spoiled. 'Don't let him cut my hand off –   *25*
The doctor, when he comes. Don't let him sister!'
So. But the hand was gone already.
The doctor put him in the dark of ether.   **ether** *an anaesthetic.*
He lay and puffed his lips out with his breath.
And then – the watcher at his pulse took fright.   *30*
No one believed. They listened at his heart.
Little – less – nothing! – and that ended it.
No more to build on there. And they, since they
Were not the one dead, turned to their affairs.

Thinking/Talking Points

▷ Why do you think Robert Frost chose those words from *Macbeth* as the title for this poem?

▷ How would you describe the mood of the opening twelve lines?
Which details help to set the scene?

▷ How does the poet suggest the sound of the saw?
What sort of 'personality' does it seem to have?

▷ Why do you think the boy gave 'a rueful laugh' immediately after the accident?

▷ What do you think the poet means when he says
'Then the boy saw all . . .
              all spoiled'?

▷ Why do you think the boy died?
How does the poet capture the moment of his death?

▷ Can you understand the reaction of the onlookers?

Read the poem again now to see what other points are worth talking about before you tackle the assignment.

Assignment

English

○ *All Spoiled.* Rewrite this story in verse or prose from the point of view of one of the onlookers.
Use details from the poem but add plenty of your own ideas. (Tell us something about the boy: his appearance, his personality. Describe the job you were doing when the accident happened. Try to share the feelings which made you turn back to your affairs when you realised the boy had died.)

Heaney
DEATH OF A NATURALIST

What do we mean when we describe a child as 'innocent'?
What do you understand by the term 'experience'?

Have there been particular moments, particular experiences in your life after which you were never quite the same again? (e.g. Do you remember when you found out the 'truth' about Father Christmas? When and where did you learn the 'facts of life'? Can you remember how you felt when you learnt some of those 'facts'? Was there a particular discovery which saddened or angered or confused you?)

Read through the following poem carefully two or three times before thinking about the points which follow.

Death of a Naturalist

All year the flax-dam festered in the heart
Of the townland; green and heavy headed
Flax had rotted there, weighted down by huge sods.
Daily it sweltered in the punishing sun.
Bubbles gargled delicately, bluebottles   5
Wove a strong gauze of sound around the smell.
There were dragon-flies, spotted butterflies,
But best of all was the warm thick slobber
Of frogspawn that grew like clotted water
In the shade of the banks. Here, every spring   10
I would fill jampotfuls of the jellied
Specks to range on window-sills at home,
On shelves at school, and wait and watch until
The fattening dots burst into nimble-
Swimming tadpoles. Miss Walls would tell us how   15
The daddy frog was called a bullfrog
And how he croaked and how the mammy frog
Laid hundreds of little eggs and this was
Frogspawn. You could tell the weather by frogs too
For they were yellow in the sun and brown   20
In rain.

   Then one hot day when fields were rank
With cowdung in the grass, the angry frogs
Invaded the flax-dam; I ducked through hedges
To a coarse croaking that I had not heard   25
Before. The air was thick with a bass chorus.

naturalist someone who
studies Nature.
flax a crop from which
linen is made.
flax-dam a stagnant pond
in which harvested flax is
left to decompose to prepare
it for manufacture.
festered rotted, fermented.
sods turfs.
sweltered sweated.
gauze of sound a haze,
a blur of sound.

rank stinking.

Right down the dam gross-bellied frogs were cocked
On sods; their loose necks pulsed like sails. Some hopped:
The slap and plop were obscene threats. Some sat
Poised like mud grenades, their blunt heads farting.   *30*
I sickened, turned, and ran. The great slime kings
Were gathered there for vengeance and I knew   **vengeance** *revenge.*
That if I dipped my hand the spawn would clutch it.

Thinking/Talking Points

▷ How would you describe the mood of the first stanza of the poem?
Which words and phrases help to create that mood? (e.g. What does the phrase
'best of all' on line 8 suggest to you about the child's feelings about Nature?)

▷ Do you think your attitude to school was different ten years ago?
Can you remember a particular episode from your primary school which
demonstrates how much you have changed?

▷ Look again at stanza 2.
How would you describe the tone of the opening sentence? Which words and
phrases describing the frogs would never have been used in Miss Walls's
lesson?

▷ What mixture of feelings do you think the boy had as he watched and then ran
away from the frogs in the flax-dam?
Why do you think the poet called this work *Death of a Naturalist*?
How would you describe what has happened to the boy?
Can you suggest an alternative title for the poem?

Read the poem again now once or twice before you choose an assignment.

Assignments

English

○ *Basic Facts*
Write a poem or a short story about a moment in a child's life when he or she
learns with a shock one of the 'facts of life'. (e.g. A pet, relative or close friend
dies; a child discovers that not everyone in the family loves everyone else; that
a parent or teacher can make mistakes; that babies aren't delivered by storks;
or that the meat in the supermarket comes from factory farms.)

English Literature

○ Essay: By looking carefully at the way the boy feels at different stages in the
poem, explain why it is called *Death of a Naturalist*.
Does the experience he describes have any parallels in your own 'growing up'?

★

= *Scannell* =
THE FAIR

Do you remember the last time you went to a fair?

Can you recall what the fairground looked like from a distance?

What mood were you in as you got nearer?

Picture yourself walking round. What special fairground sounds and smells can you remember?

Do you remember the expressions on people's faces as they giggled and screamed and enjoyed themselves?

Can you recall a particular moment of panic or delight?

Read through the following poem carefully two or three times before thinking about the points which follow.

The Fair

Music and yellow steam, the fizz
Of spinning lights as roundabouts
Galloping nowhere whirl and whizz
Through fusillades of squeals and shouts;
The night sniffs rich at pungent spice,   5
Brandysnap and diesel oil;
The stars like scattered beads of rice
Sparsely fleck the sky's deep soil
Dulled and diminished by these trapped
Melodic meteors below   10
In whose feigned fever brightly lapped
The innocent excitements flow.
Pocketfuls of simple thrills
Jingle silver, purchasing
A warm and sugared fear that spills   15
From dizzy car and breathless swing.
So no one hears the honest shriek
From the field beyond the fair,
A single voice becoming weak,
Then dying on the ignorant air.   20
And not for hours will frightened love
Rise and seek her everywhere,
Then find her, like a fallen glove,
Soiled and crumpled, lying there.

fusillades usually, a
barrage of rifle fire.
pungent strongly smelling.

diminished made to look
smaller.

feigned fever false, phoney
excitement.
lapped surrounded.

☆

Thinking/Talking Points

▷ Notice how many different fairground sounds the poet captures.
How many fairground smells has he described?
Which of those can you 'smell' as you read about them?
And of all the pictures he paints, which do you think best captures the movement, the excitement, the magic of a fairground?

▷ Look at lines 7–12 again.
See if you can express that idea in your own words.

▷ What exactly is the difference between the 'warm and sugared fear' (lines 15–16) and the 'honest shriek' (see lines 17–20)?

▷ Look at the poem's final two lines.
Can you explain why the girl is described in that way?

Assignments

English

○ Using some of the ideas in this poem, but also your own memories of fairgrounds and your imagination, write the *opening page* of a short story which is to be about a murder committed at a fair.
The page you write should be concerned with describing the fair in the way that a child who is going for the first time to a fair, alone, might experience it. Try to make your reader share all the colour and noise, smells, laughter, confusion, excitement and fun of the fair. But see if you can also suggest a hint of real menace in the situation.

English Literature

○ Essay: With close reference to the text, show how Vernon Scannell generates first one mood then another in *The Fair*. Which details did you find particularly effective?

★

═══ *Thomas* ═══
FERN HILL

What do you feel are the most important differences between children and adults?

Where do you think you belong? Do you think being a teenager is more like being a child, or more like being an adult?

Do you think you were a very different person when you were six?

How would you describe the difference between behaviour which is 'child-like' and behaviour which is 'childish'? Jot down some examples of each.

When you recall your own early childhood, what sights and sounds and smells, what games, what experiences pass through your mind? (e.g. Was the sun always shining? Was the world a kind place?)

Do you remember how you felt about 'adults' then?

Can you remember what you thought it would be like to be sixteen?

What ideas, ways of seeing the world, were beyond you as a child? (e.g. Were you interested in the news? Did you think about a career or about marriage? Can you remember ever thinking about time or death?)

What do you think is responsible for your losing your child-like self?

When did you first have 'responsibilities', 'duties', 'obligations'?

When do you think you will be an 'adult'?

Do you think you will be very different then?

Read through the following poem carefully a few times and give yourself time to relate it to some of the things we have already considered before looking at the points which follow.

Fern Hill

Now as I was young and easy under the apple boughs
About the lilting house and happy as the grass was green,
   The night above the dingle starry,
     Time let me hail and climb
   Golden in the heydays of his eyes,
And honoured among wagons I was prince of the apple towns
And once below a time I lordly had the trees and leaves
    Trail with daisies and barley
   Down the rivers of the windfall light.

lilting singing.

dingle narrow wooded valley.

5 *heydays* prime, best days.

And as I was green and carefree, famous among the barns   *10*
About the happy yard and singing as the farm was home,
   In the sun that is young once only,
     Time let me play and be
   Golden in the mercy of his means,
And green and golden I was huntsman and herdsman, the calves *15*
Sang to my horn, the foxes on the hills barked clear and cold,
   And the sabbath rang slowly
   In the pebbles of the holy streams.

All the sun long it was running, it was lovely, the hay
Fields high as the house, the tunes from the chimneys, it was air *20*
   And playing, lovely and watery
     And fire green as grass.
   And nightly under the simple stars
As I rode to sleep the owls were bearing the farm away,
All the moon long I heard, blessed among stables, the nightjars *25*
   Flying with the ricks, and the horses
     Flashing into the dark.

And then to awake, and the farm, like a wanderer white
With the dew, come back, the cock on his shoulder: it was all
   Shining, it was Adam and maiden,   *30*
     The sky gathered again
   And the sun grew round that very day.
So it must have been after the birth of the simple light
In the first, spinning place, the spellbound horses walking warm
   Out of the whinnying green stable   *35*
     On to the fields of praise.

And honoured among foxes and pheasants by the gay house
Under the new made clouds and happy as the heart was long,
   In the sun born over and over,
     I ran my heedless ways,   *40*
   My wishes raced through the house high hay
And nothing I cared, at my sky blue trades, that time allows
In all his tuneful turning so few and such morning songs
   Before the children green and golden
     Follow him out of grace.   *45*

Nothing I cared, in the lamb white days, that time would take me
Up to the swallow thronged loft by the shadow of my hand,
   In the moon that is always rising,
     Nor that riding to sleep
   I should hear him fly with the high fields   *50*
Oh as I was young and easy in the mercy of his means,
   Time held me green and dying
   Though I sang in my chains like the sea.

☆

sabbath *day of rest, day of worship.*

nightjar *nocturnal bird.*
ricks *stacks of corn.*

heedless *carefree.*

grace *innocence.*

Thinking/Talking Points

▷ What kind of voice do you hear reading the poem?

▷ What is the connection between the mood of the first two lines and their length?

▷ 'young and easy . . .' is a sort of half-echo of the everyday phrase 'free and easy'; the poet is packing his ideas into as few words as possible.
What familiar phrases do you hear half-echoed in: 'happy as the grass was green' and 'once below a time'?
What ideas is the poet combining in these phrases?
See if you can find further examples of this technique.

▷ 'lilting house . . . happy yard . . . holy streams'
What child-like way of seeing the world do these phrases suggest to you?
Can you find other examples of the poet showing us the world through the child's eyes?

▷ How many details of the story of Adam and Eve in the Garden of Eden can you remember?
Why did the couple have to leave the Garden?
Was that a good thing as well as a bad thing?
See how many echoes of that story you can find in *Fern Hill*. (e.g. In what ways is the farm like Paradise? In what senses is the child like Adam before he ate the forbidden fruit?)

▷ How often is 'Time' mentioned in the poem?
What do you notice about the lines in which Time figures?
Can you explain how an adult's sense of Time is different from a child's?
Have you noticed your own notion of Time changing as you have got older?

▷ Look again at stanza 3.
What seems to happen when the child sleeps?
What do you associate with owls? And with the moon?
Can you suggest what the child is being given a glimpse of here?
                              'the nightjars
Flying with the ricks, and the horses
Flashing into the dark.'?

▷ Read the last two stanzas of the poem again.
Can you explain what it is that leads the child out of innocence?
When do you think the speaker realised he was 'in . . . chains'?
How 'free and easy' do you feel you are now?

Reread the poem carefully now to see what else deserves attention before you choose your assignment.

Assignments

English

○ *Looking Back*
Write, in verse or prose, about yourself as you were as a young child.
Concentrate upon a particular place or one particular experience you

remember vividly and try to recapture the child-like wonder, fears, drama, optimism, confusions, anxieties and joys you felt then.

Here is a prose piece 'written under the Thomas influence' by a fifteen-year-old recalling his primary school.

Greenways

Then it was the fear of the complicated songs in the morning and the wooden toys in the afternoon. The squeak of plimsolls on hard wooden floors. Stale milk bottles in a crate. The winged mirror's cold, remote hand saying 'Are those spiders or suns? Look like spiders. Funny kind of Easter card I call it . . .'

There was the fight for the big red wooden engine which I always avoided. Scrammed cheek and maimed pride, 'Miss gave it me!' not healed by all the adult shouting about 'Blood on his handkerchief!'

Then came the long, lonely walk home across a giant park under endless blue sky; bright white shorts against dull orange sand as sulphur yellow balls slammed and zinged into rusting diamond wire. Roger and his tall dog; the old lady without teeth, emptying her tealeaves in the garden.

Thom Wilson

○ *Hello Stranger*

Imagine discovering, in thirty or forty years' time, a photograph taken of you this year.

What might your fifty-year-old self feel looking back to when he/she was the age you are now?

What might he/she envy, regret, be critical of?

What would he/she make of your attitudes, worries, hopes and frustrations? Your friends? Your clothes? . . .

What particular memories of being a teenager do you think your fifty-year-old self will treasure?

See if you can write a poem or piece of prose about yourself seen from the perspective of a much older person.

English Literature

○ Essay: 'Out of Grace'.

With close reference to the text, examine the ways Dylan Thomas explores the theme of the loss of childhood innocence in *Fern Hill*.

Do you have similar feelings about the process of growing up?

Further reading

Thomas	*Portrait of the Artist as a Young Dog* (especially *The Peaches*; *A Visit to Grandpa's; The Fight*)
	Reminiscences of Childhood
	Holiday Memory
	Memories of Christmas
Mark	*Nothing To Be Afraid Of*
Milne	*When We Were Very Young*
McGough/Rosen	*You Tell Me*

★

THE JAGUAR
and
SECOND GLANCE AT A JAGUAR

'A robin redbreast in a cage
Puts all Heaven in a rage.'

William Blake (1757–1827)

Can you remember visiting a zoo?
Which creatures seemed most/least comfortable in captivity?
Which animals fascinated you?
What did they look like? How did they behave?

If you could be any wild animal, what would it be?
How would that animal feel behind bars?

Read through the following poem carefully two or three times before thinking
about the points which follow.

The Jaguar

The apes yawn and adore their fleas in the sun.
The parrots shriek as if they were on fire, or strut   **strut** *parade, show off.*
Like cheap tarts to attract the stroller with the nut.
Fatigued with indolence, tiger and lion   **fatigued with indolence**
                                             worn out with doing
Lie still as the sun. The boa-constrictor's coil   5   *nothing.*
Is a fossil. Cage after cage seems empty, or
Stinks of sleepers from the breathing straw.
It might be painted on a nursery wall.

But who runs like the rest past these arrives
At a cage where the crowd stands, stares, mesmerized,   10   **mesmerized** *fascinated,*
As a child at a dream, at a jaguar hurrying enraged   *hypnotised.*
Through prison darkness after the drills of his eyes

On a short fierce fuse. Not in boredom –
The eye satisfied to be blind in fire,
By the bang of blood in the brain deaf the ear –   15
He spins from the bars, but there's no cage to him

More than to the visionary his cell: **visionary** *prophet, mystic,*
His stride is wildernesses of freedom: *dreamer.*
The world rolls under the long thrust of his heel.
Over the cage floor the horizons come.

☆   25

Thinking/Talking Points

▷ Look again at the first two stanzas.
Which details give you the most vivid sense of the zoo's atmosphere?
Suggest why the poet chose to split this sentence across two stanzas:
'Fatigued with indolence, tiger and lion
Lie still as the sun.'

▷ How do you imagine the crowd around the jaguar's cage – their expressions, their comments, the way they stand?

▷ Which details describing the jaguar impress you?
Suggest some words or phrases of your own to sum up the animal's character.

▷ What do you think the poet means when he says:
'there's no cage to him
More than to the visionary his cell'?

▷ See if you can put the last line of the poem into your own words.

Read the poem again now before you choose an assignment.

Assignments

English

○ Draw a picture of Hughes's jaguar.

○ In verse or prose, write about a visit to the zoo.
Begin by describing the atmosphere of the place, the weather and the people milling around you.
Then describe three or four rather dull specimens and finally the one which fixes all your attention.
Try to capture the animal's appearance, movements and character.
Should this creature be behind bars?

○ Imagine yourself as a creature in a zoo.
Write a piece of verse or prose in which you describe and reflect upon your lifestyle – perhaps comparing it with your days in the wild.
What do you make of your fellow inmates? And of the humans who come and pay to stare at you?

English Literature

○ Essay: Below is another poem by Hughes, *Second Glance at a Jaguar*. Compare and contrast Hughes's two poems. Which details in each poem best capture the character of the beast?
What qualities in the jaguar does the poet most admire?
Do you prefer one poem to the other? Why?

Second Glance at a Jaguar

Skinful of bowls, he bowls them,
The hip going in and out of joint, dropping the spine
With the urgency of his hurry
Like a cat going under thrown stones, under cover,
Glancing sideways, running   5
Under his spine. A terrible, stump-legged waddle
Like a thick Aztec disemboweller,
Club-swinging, trying to grind some square
Socket between his hind legs round,
Carrying his head like a brazier of spilling embers,   10
And the black bit of his mouth, he takes it
Between his back teeth, he has to wear his skin out,
He swipes a lap at the water-trough as he turns,
Swivelling a ball of his heel on the polished spot,
Showing his belly like a butterfly,   15
At every stride he has to turn a corner
In himself and correct it. His head
Is like the worn down stump of another whole jaguar,
His body is just the engine shoving it forward,
Lifting the air up and shoving on under,   20
The weight of his fangs hanging the mouth open,
Bottom jaw combing the ground. A gorged look,
Gangster, club-tail lumped along behind gracelessly,
He's wearing himself to heavy ovals,
Muttering some mantrah, some drum-song of murder   25
To keep his rage brightening, making his skin
Intolerable, spurred by the rosettes, the cain-brands,
Wearing the spots off from the inside,
Rounding some revenge. Going like a prayer-wheel,
The head dragging forward, the body keeping up,   30
The hind legs lagging. He coils, he flourishes
The blackjack tail, as if looking for a target,
Hurrying through the underworld, soundless.

thick thick-set, squat.
Aztec disemboweller member of an ancient Mexican tribe which tore out the guts of their enemies.
brazier a firebasket.
embers bits of glowing coal or wood from a fire.

gorged glutted, over-full.

mantrah incantation, a prayer repeated over and over again.
drum-song primitive warrior's song.
cain-brands marks inherited from Cain, the first murderer.
prayer-wheel a gadget used by Tibetan Buddhists on which written prayers are rotated instead of being spoken.
flourishes flaunts, brandishes.
blackjack a leather-covered club with a weighted head and a flexible shaft.
underworld criminal world; Hell.

★

= *Lawrence* =
SNAKE

What pictures do you see, what feelings do you have when you hear the word 'snake'?
What sort of snake do you think of?
Has it a particular colour and texture, a particular way of moving?
Have you ever handled a snake? If so, did the experience change the way you felt about them?
With what kinds of *human* behaviour is the snake associated?

Read through the following poem carefully two or three times before looking at the points which follow.

Snake

A snake came to my water-trough
On a hot, hot day, and I in pyjamas for the heat,
To drink there.

In the deep, strange-scented shade of the great dark carob tree
I came down the steps with my pitcher   5
And must wait, must stand and wait, for there he was at the
                                   trough before me.

He reached down from a fissure in the earth-wall in the gloom
And trailed his yellow-brown slackness soft-bellied down,
                       over the edge of the stone trough
And rested his throat upon the stone bottom,
And where the water had dripped from the tap, in a small
                                  clearness,   *10*
He sipped with his straight mouth,
Softly drank through his straight gums, into his slack long body,
Silently.

Someone was before me at my water-trough,
And I, like a second-comer, waiting.   *15*

He lifted his head from his drinking, as cattle do,
And looked at me vaguely, as drinking cattle do,
And flickered his two-forked tongue from his lips, and mused
                                  a moment,
And stooped and drank a little more,
Being earth-brown, earth-golden from the burning bowels of
                             the earth   *20*
On the day of Sicilian July, with Etna smoking.

carob tree (locust tree) an evergreen which grows in the Mediterranean region.
pitcher large earthenware pot.
trough water container.
fissure split, crack.

mused reflected.

burning bowels of the earth the fiery centre of the earth.
Etna a volcano in eastern Sicily.

28

The voice of my education said to me
He must be killed,
For in Sicily the black, black snakes are innocent, the gold are
venomous,   **venomous** *poisonous.*

And voices in me said, If you were a man   25
You would take a stick and break him now, and finish him off.

But must I confess how I liked him,
How glad I was he had come like a guest in quiet, to drink at my
water-trough
And depart peaceful, pacified, and thankless,
Into the burning bowels of this earth?   30

Was it cowardice, that I dared not kill him?
Was it perversity, that I longed to talk to him?   **perversity** *stubborn*
Was it humility, to feel so honoured?   *oddness.*
I felt so honoured.   **humility** *respect, meekness.*

And yet those voices: 35
If you were not afraid, you would kill him!

And truly I was afraid, I was most afraid,
But even so, honoured still more
That he should seek my hospitality
From out the dark door of the secret earth.   40

He drank enough
And lifted his head, dreamily, as one who has drunken,
And flickered his tongue like a forked night on the air, so black;
Seeming to lick his lips,
And looked around like a god, unseeing, into the air   45
And slowly turned his head,
And slowly, very slowly, as if thrice adream,
Proceeded to draw his slow length curving round
And climb again the broken bank of my wall-face.

And as he put his head into that dreadful hole,   50
And as he slowly drew up, snake-easing his shoulders, and
entered farther,
A sort of horror, a sort of protest against his withdrawing into
that horrid black hole,
Deliberately going into the blackness, and slowly drawing
himself after,
Overcame me now his back was turned.

I looked round, I put down my pitcher,   55
I picked up a clumsy log
And threw it at the water-trough with a clatter.

I think it did not hit him,
But suddenly that part of him that was left behind convulsed in
                                        undignified haste,
Writhed like lightning, and was gone   60   **writhed** *wriggled,*
Into the black hole, the earth-lipped fissure in the wall-front,   *squirmed.*
At which, in the intense still noon, I stared with fascination.

And immediately I regretted it.
I thought how paltry, how vulgar, what a mean act!   **paltry** *mean-spirited, petty.*
I despised myself and the voices of my accursed human   **vulgar** *crude, barbaric.*
                                        education.   65

And I thought of the albatross,   **albatross** *this is the bird*
And I wished he would come back, my snake.   *in Coleridge's poem* The
                                                              Ancient Mariner *whose*
                                                              killing brings bad luck.
For he seemed to me again like a king,
Like a king in exile, uncrowned in the underworld,
Now due to be crowned again.   70

And so, I missed my chance with one of the lords
Of life.
And I have something to expiate: **expiate** *atone for, make*
A pettiness.   *amends for.*

Thinking/Talking Points

▷   Do you feel the speaker's behaviour was understandable, excusable?
    How do you think *you* might have behaved in the circumstances?

▷   How does Lawrence capture the snake's movements in words?
    Which phrases do you find most suggestive?
    What is the effect of the long lines of verse?
    Why do you think 'silently' has the whole of line 13 to itself?

▷   Which details of this snake's appearance and behaviour make him seem most
    alien, sub-human?
    Which details suggest a super-human creature?

▷   What do you understand by the phrase 'The voice of my education' (line 22)?
    What other 'voices' does the poet hear?

▷   Can you describe in your own words the contradictory feelings passing through
    the speaker's mind in lines 31–40?

▷   What finally stirs the speaker into action?
    How does he feel about what he did?
    What exactly do you think Lawrence means by the 'pettiness' of his action?

▷   What were your own feelings about this particular visitor by the end of the
    poem?

    Read the poem again now to see what other points need thinking about before
    you choose an assignment.

Assignments

English

○ Compose a poem or a piece of prose exploring a similar mixture of feelings about some creature (e.g. a spider; a worm; a beetle; a crow; a bat; a crocodile; a toad).

○ Essay: Would you agree that a lack of respect for other creatures lowers a person's self-esteem? (You may wish to write about experiments on living animals, about factory-farming or about whether people should be allowed to kill animals for 'sport'.)

English Literature

○ 'Lawrence's *Snake*: an appreciation'.
Write a study of this poem, bringing out Lawrence's changing feelings about his visitor. Remember to refer closely to the text in your answer.

Further reading

Lawrence   Essay   *Reflections on the Death of a Porcupine*
              Poems   *Man and Bat; Mosquito*

★

The Thought-Fox

I imagine this midnight moment's forest:
Something else is alive
Beside the clock's loneliness
And this blank page where my fingers move.

Through the window I see no star: *5*
Something more near
Though deeper within darkness
Is entering the loneliness:

Cold, delicately as the dark snow,
A fox's nose touches twig, leaf;   *10*
Two eyes serve a movement, that now
And again now, and now, and now

Sets neat prints into the snow
Between trees, and warily a lame
Shadow lags by stump and in hollow   *15*
Of a body that is bold to come

Across clearings, an eye,
A widening deepening greenness,
Brilliantly, concentratedly,
Coming about its own business   *20*

Till, with a sudden sharp hot stink of fox
It enters the dark hole of the head.
The window is starless still; the clock ticks,
The page is printed.

Thinking/Talking Points

▷   Put yourself in the poet's place. Sit at his desk.
    How do you imagine the atmosphere in 'this midnight moment's forest'?
    Where are you? What can you hear? Are you alone?

▷   Why is the page 'blank'? Describe those fingers.
    What's the temperature in the room?

▷ What is reflected in the window as you try to stare out?

▷ How do you become aware of 'Something . . . entering the loneliness'?

▷ How deep is the snow? What sort of tracks does the thought-fox make?

▷ What is the fox's mood when you first catch sight of it?
What gives it confidence to advance?

▷ How do you know when the fox is almost unbearably close?
How does that make you feel?

▷ Why 'Thought-Fox' and not just 'Fox'?
What has been happening to the blank page?

Reread *The Thought-Fox* to see what other points need thinking about before you choose your assignment.

Assignments

English

○ *Thought-* ✳✳✳✳✳✳
What else is outside the window, waiting to advance?
See if you can capture in verse or prose another animal, bird or insect.

English Literature

○ Essay: 'As we read the poem, we experience at the same time the living approach of the fox and the firing of the poet's imagination.'
By looking at the text in detail, show how that is achieved.

○ Essay: Compare and contrast Ted Hughes's poem with the one below by Thomas Hardy.
Do you prefer one poem to the other? Can you say why?
Refer closely to the texts in your answer.

An August Midnight

I

A shaded lamp and a waving blind,
And the beat of a clock from a distant floor:
On this scene enter – winged, horned and spined –
A longlegs, a moth, and a dumbledore;
While 'mid my page there idly stands   5
A sleepy fly, that rubs its hands . . .

dumbledore *a cockchafer (an ungainly flying beetle).*

II

Thus meet we five, in this still place,
At this point of time, at this point in space.
– My guests besmear my new-penned line,
Or bang at the lamp and fall supine.   10
'God's humblest, they!' I muse. Yet why?
They know Earth-secrets that know not I.

besmear *smear.*
supine *helpless on their backs.*
muse *reflect.*

★

RAIN

Picture a cold, wintery afternoon of pounding downpour.

Imagine yourself working outside – gardening, trying to fix a car, building
something or working on a market stall.
How would your clothes feel, your hair, your hands?
What would make the job so difficult?
What mood might you be in?

Jot down a few words and phrases to set such a scene.

Read through the following poem carefully two or three times before
considering the points which follow.

Rain

Rain. Floods. Frost. And after frost, rain.
Dull roof-drumming. Wraith-rain pulsing across purple-bare
                           woods
Like light across heaved water. Sleet in it.
And the poor fields, miserable tents of their hedges.
Mist-rain off world. Hills wallowing   5
In and out of a grey or silvery dissolution. A farm gleaming,
Then all dull in the near drumming. At field-corners
Brown water backing and brimming in grass.
Toads hop across rain-hammered roads. Every mutilated leaf
                           there
Looks like a frog or a rained-out mouse. Cattle   10
Wait under blackened backs. We drive post-holes.
They half fill with water before the post goes in.
Mud-water spurts as the iron bar slam-burns
The oak stake-head dry. Cows
Tamed on the waste mudded like a rugby field   15
Stand and watch, come very close for company
In the rain that goes on and on, and gets colder.
They sniff the wire, sniff the tractor, watch. The hedges
Are straggles of gap. A few haws. Every half-ton cow
Sinks to the fetlock at every sliding stride.   20
They are ruining their field and they know it.
They look out sideways from under their brows which are
Their only shelter. The sunk scrubby wood
Is a pulverised wreck, rain riddles its holes
To the drowned roots. A pheasant looking black   25
In his waterproofs, bends at his job in the stubble.

Glosses:

wraith-rain *faint, pale, ghostly rain.*

wallowing *rolling about.*
dissolution *dissolving into liquid.*

haws *hawthorn berries.*
fetlock *part of the leg behind and just above the hoof.*

pulverised *destroyed, reduced to powder/pulp.*
riddles *bores through.*

The mid-afternoon dusk soaks into
The soaked thickets. Nothing protects them.
The fox corpses lie beaten to their bare bones,
Skin beaten off, brains and bowels beaten out.　　　30　　**bowels** *guts.*
Nothing but their blueprint bones last in the rain,
Sodden soft. Round their hay racks, calves　　　　　　**sodden** *saturated.*
Stand in a shine of mud. The gateways
Are deep obstacles of mud. The calves look up, through
　　　　　　　　　　　　　　plastered forelocks,
Without moving. Nowhere they can go.　　　　　　35
Is less uncomfortable. The brimming world
And the pouring sky are the only places
For them to be. Fieldfares squeal over, sodden　　　**fieldfares** *thrushlike birds.*
Toward the sodden wood. A raven,
Cursing monotonously, goes over fast　　　　　　40
And vanishes in rain-mist. Magpies
Shake themselves hopelessly, hop in the spatter. Misery.　　**spatter** *shower.*
Surviving green of ferns and brambles is tumbled
Like an abandoned scrapyard. The calves
Wait deep beneath their spines. Cows roar　　　　45
Then hang their noses to the mud.
Snipe go over, invisible in the dusk,　　　　　**snipe** *marshland bird with*
With their squelching cries.　　　　　　　　　　　*long bill.*

Thinking/Talking Points

▷　How do you picture the speaker?
　What tone(s) of voice do you hear in the poem?
　Why do you think there are so many short, broken sentences?

▷　Notice how many different creatures are mentioned in the poem.
　Which phrases describing them do you think are effective?

▷　Which words and phrases do you think best capture the sound, the appearance
　and the feel of the rain?
　How does the speaker emphasise its never-ending monotony?

▷　Suggest what the phrase 'blueprint bones' (line 31) means.

　Look at the poem again now to see what else makes the poem memorable
　before you choose your assignment.

Assignments

English

(a) Pick out the details which did most to convey to you the atmosphere of this particular day in this particular place.
If the poem had been about a scorching day in the middle of June, what details might have been used in their place? Write down as many as you can.

(b) Write a piece called 'Drought': either an unrhymed poem like this one or a piece of prose.
Use the same location and as many of the same creatures as seem appropriate.
The speaker should be doing a similar farm job too.
Try to give the reader the feeling that he/she is there, suffering the dry heat, the searing light, the unrelenting pressure of the day.
Show how the animals are affected too.

You may like to try making a line-for-line 'translation' of Ted Hughes's poem.

English Literature

○ Write an appreciation of *Rain*, describing how the poet shared this particular experience with us.
What did you most like/dislike about the poem?
Remember to refer closely to the text in your answer.

★

Read through the following poem carefully three or four times before thinking about the points which follow.

Spinster

Now this particular girl
During a ceremonious April walk
With her latest suitor
Found herself, of a sudden, intolerably struck
By the birds' irregular babel   5
And the leaves' litter.

By this tumult afflicted, she
Observed her lover's gestures unbalance the air,
Her gait stray uneven
Through a rank wilderness of fern and flower.   10
She judged petals in disarray,
The whole season sloven.

How she longed for winter then! –
Scrupulously austere in its order
Of white and black   15
Ice and rock, each sentiment within border,
And heart's frosty discipline
Exact as a snowflake.

But here – a burgeoning
Unruly enough to pitch her five queenly wits   20
Into vulgar motley –
A treason not to be borne. Let idiots
Reel giddy in bedlam spring:
She withdrew neatly.

And round her house she set   25
Such a barricade of barb and check
Against mutinous weather
As no mere insurgent man could hope to break
With curse, fist, threat
Or love, either.

☆

spinster *an unmarried woman.*
ceremonious *formal, stately, very correct and polite.*
babel *meaningless chatter.*

tumult *noise.*
afflicted *upset, distressed.*
gait *way of walking.*
rank *overgrown, coarse, loathsome, indecent.*
sloven *untidy, dirty, unkempt.*

scrupulously austere *punctilious, careful to the smallest detail in being strict, simple, pure.*
order *(i) precise arrangement (ii) a religious community with strict rules.*
sentiment *feeling.*
burgeoning *blossoming, budding, breaking into new growth.*
unruly *undisciplined.*
vulgar motley *dressed/ behaving like a common fool.*
bedlam *crazy, confused, unruly.*

insurgent *invading, trying to overthrow, threatening.*

Thinking/Talking Points

Do not write full answers to these questions; some notes may be helpful when you plan your assignment.

▷ What do we mean when we say somebody 'sees things in black and white'? What sort of temperament does such a person have? How would you feel if you were ordered to wear only black and white clothes?

▷ Can you suggest more than one meaning of the phrase, 'this particular girl'? Suggest a few words of your own to describe her.

▷ In what season is the poem set? What thoughts, feelings and activities do you associate with that time of year?

▷ What is the spinster's favourite season? Why?

▷ How would you explain the connection between the girl's attitude to the seasons and her attitude to 'her latest suitor'?

▷ What does she decide to do about him?

▷ What do you think the *poet's* attitude to the girl is and to the choice she makes? (Think particularly about how these words and phrases shape our attitude towards her: afflicted; judged; scrupulously austere; white and black; heart's frosty discipline; queenly wits; withdrew neatly; barricade; or love, either.)

Reread *Spinster* now a couple of times to see what else deserves attention before you choose your assignment. Think about the tone of voice in which it would be most effective to read the poem aloud.

Assignments

English

○ In verse or prose, write an account of that April day, either from the point of view of the girl or from the point of view of her suitor. Draw on the details from the poem but add plenty of ideas of your own to try to bring the speaker vividly alive before the reader.

English Literature·

○ Essay: 'It is not just love but life itself from which this nun-like spinster withdraws.' Do you agree? Write an appreciation of *Spinster*, showing how the poet has shaped our attitude to her subject. Do you feel sorry for the girl? Why? Remember to refer closely to the text in your answer.

For further reading

Shakespeare   *Measure for Measure* Act I sc. iv

★

LOVE IS . . .
and
WITHOUT YOU

Love Is . . .

Love is feeling cold in the back of vans
Love is a fanclub with only two fans
Love is walking holding paintstained hands
Love is

Love is fish and chips on winter nights   5
Love is blankets full of strange delights
Love is when you don't put out the light
Love is

Love is the presents in the Christmas shops
Love is when you're feeling Top of the Pops   10
Love is what happens when the music stops
Love is

Love is white panties lying all forlorn
Love is a pink nightdress still slightly warm
Love is when you have to leave at dawn   15
Love is

Love is you and love is me
Love is a prison and love is free
Love's what's there when you're away from me
Love is . . .

☆

Without You

Without you every morning would be like going back to work after a holiday,
Without you I couldn't stand the smell of the East Lancs Road,
Without you ghost ferries would cross the Mersey manned by skeleton crews,
Without you I'd probably feel happy and have more money and time and nothing
                       to do with it,
Without you I'd have to leave my stillborn poems on other people's doorsteps,
                       wrapped in brown paper,   5
Without you there'd never be sauce to put on sausage butties,

Without you plastic flowers in shop windows would just be plastic flowers in shop
windows
Without you I'd spend my summers picking morosely over the remains of train
crashes,
Without you white birds would wrench themselves free from my paintings and fly
off dripping blood into the night,
Without you green apples wouldn't taste greener, *10*
Without you Mothers wouldn't let their children out to play after tea,
Without you every musician in the world would forget how to play the blues,
Without you Public Houses would be public again,
Without you the Sunday Times colour supplement would come out in black and
white,
Without you indifferent colonels would shrug their shoulders and press the button, *15*
Without you they'd stop changing the flowers in Piccadilly Gardens,
Without you Clark Kent would forget how to become Superman,
Without you Sunshine Breakfast would only consist of Cornflakes,
Without you there'd be no colour in Magic colouring books
Without you Mahler's 8th would only be performed by street musicians in derelict
houses, *20*
Without you they'd forget to put the salt in every packet of crisps,
Without you it would be an offence punishable by a fine of up to £200 or two
months imprisonment to be found in possession of curry powder,
Without you riot police are massing in quiet sidestreets,
Without you all streets would be one-way the other way,
Without you there'd be no one not to kiss goodnight when we quarrel, *25*
Without you the first Martian to land would turn round and go away again,
Without you they'd forget to change the weather,
Without you blind men would sell unlucky heather,
Without you there would be
no landscapes/no stations/no houses,
no chipshops/no quiet villages/no seagulls
on beaches/no hopscotch on pavements/no
night/no morning/there'd be no city no country
Without you.

Assignments

English

○ Compose your own version of either (or both) of the poems.

○ Make a collage picture or cartoon to illustrate one of the poems.

★

THE YOUNG SOLDIER
WITH BLOODY SPURS

McAuley
THE SEDUCTION

Read through the following poem carefully a couple of times before considering the questions that follow.

The Young Soldier with Bloody Spurs

A servant-girl speaks

The sergeant says that eight and twenty wagons
Are coming behind, and we must put out all
The water we can at the gate, for the horses. He gallops
To the next farm, pulls up where the elder flowers fall.

The wheat on both sides of the road stands green,   *5*
And hundreds of soldiers on horseback have filed between
It, gone by our farm to the mountains that stand black blue
This morning.

               I think perhaps the man that came
To Wolfrathausen last winter's end, comes through   *10*   **Wolfrathausen** *a place in*
This place to-day. These soldiers wear the same   *South Bavaria.*
Helmets as his he lost in the wood that night,
And their uniforms are the same of white and blue –

It was cold, and he put his cloak right round me
As we walked; dark, so he held his arm close round me.   *15*
In the stillness, he took off his helmet to kiss me –
It snowed, and his helmet was lost, he forgot me, he did not
                                  miss me.

The Isar whispers again in the valley; the children   **Isar** *a river in Bavaria.*
Are ducking their heads in the water tubs at the gate
As they go from school; some of the officers rally   *20*
At the door of the Gasthaus down the road: great   **Gasthaus** *guesthouse.*
Threads of blue wind far and down the road
I wait for the eight and twenty wagons to come.

At last I hear a rattle, and there away
Crawls the first load into sight – and now there are some   *25*
Drawing near, they cover the München road.   **München** *Munich.*

                                                    Nay
I dread him coming; I wonder how he will take it.
I can see his raging black eyes blaze at me
And feel him gripping my wrist as if he would break it.   *30*

Here comes the first of the wagons, a grey, a dreary
Shut-up coffin of a thing, with a soldier weary   **box** *driver's seat.*
In the box, and four hot horses going drearily,
And a soldier in the saddle of the left-hand draught-horse,   **draught-horse** *strong*
                                sitting wearily.   *horse for pulling heavy*
                                                                 loads.

One by one they go by — at last   *35*
There he sits in the saddle of this the five
And twentieth wagon. And he will not drive past
He pulls up for our water; would he drive
On if he knew that *I* was at this farm?

And he swings his heavy thigh   *40*
Out of the saddle, and staggering
With stiffness comes for the water that I
Have poured for the horses — a dark-blue, staggering
Strong young man. He leans sighing
With head against the shaft, and takes   *45*
His helmet off, and wipes his hair, trying
To ease himself in his clothes. It makes
Me want to cry, to see him so strong and easy
Swarthy and strong with his damp thick hair   **swarthy** *dark-coloured.*
Pushed up on end — and the breath sighing   *50*
Between his thick lips. I wonder where
He thinks I am — if ever he thinks at all.
But his handkerchief is white with a broad blue border,
A nice one, I like it. He'll think it's a tall order
When I say he ought to marry me. And small   *55*
I feel I have to tell him.

                                But why, before
He waters the horses does he wash his heel?
Jesus — his spurs are red with shining blood!
He splashes water from the pail upon them,   *60*
And rubs the silver clean with his thick brown fingers,
Bending backwards awkwardly,
And anxiously, like a boy afraid to be found out.

And he goes and washes the belly of his horse,
A poor roan thing: its hind leg twitches   *65*   **roan** *bay or dark colour*
Forwards as he rubs the wound   *with grey or white spots.*
And bloody water falls upon the road
Soiling the clean white dust. He rubs the belly
Carefully again, and again, to stop the bleeding.
Jesus — his fingers are red!   *70*
And again, rolling in his heavy high boots,

43

He comes to the side of the road and washes his hand,
And looks round again at his heel, the bright spur,
And bends again and looks at the belly of the horse,
And kicks dust over the red stain in the road.   75
And all the time his handsome, swarthy red face
With savage black eyes is sulky: and all the time
He frowns as if he were worried, as if the place
On the horse's belly hurt him, for he was rather gentle
To the thing, and rather fretted. And his thick black hair   80
Was wet with sweat, and his movements strong and heavy.
– I wonder, will he care!

Now I take the big stone jug of water
Down to the gate, and stand and wait
For a word. He is coming towards the gate –   85
His eyes meet mine as he takes the jug of water.
He knows me, but does not speak: instead
He drinks and drinks, then turns away his head.

'Do you remember me?'
– 'Yes!'   90
'Who then?'
– 'Maria, of the Gasthaus Green Hat, Wolfrathausen.'
'I am with child by you –'
He looked at me, and his heavy brows came over
His eyes and he sulked. He had another lover.   95

'It is true,' I said.
– 'And what do you want?'
'What do you think?' I said.

He looked away down the road.

Suddenly his horses began to start.   100   **start** *shy away.*
He shouted, ran heavily after them,
And jerked back their bridles, pushing their heads apart
I waited, but he would not come back to me
He stayed with the horses, sulkily,
Till the whistle went. Then swiftly he   105
Swung strong and heavy to saddle again
And called to his horses, and his strong blue body
Had its back to me;
And away went the last of the wagons.

☆

Thinking/Talking Points

▷   What impression of the girl's personality and situation does the first stanza give
you?
How do you think she feels about the soldiers?

▷ Which detail first establishes the connection between the girl and the unnamed young man?

▷ What does the *way* the girl tells us about what happened 'that night' (lines 14–17) suggest about her feelings now?
Do you think she sounds sorry for herself?

▷ What do you think the girl feels as the wagons approach?
What does she know about her soldier's personality?

▷ Look again at lines 40–56.
Which details suggest the young man's temperament most vividly?

▷ What impact did lines 57–63 make upon you?
What does the line
'And anxiously, like a boy afraid to be found out'
reveal about what he has done? And about his attitude to it?

▷ Read lines 64–82 again.
How does Lawrence make us feel sympathy for the horse?
Which details here add to our picture of the soldier?

▷ Now look again at lines 83 to the end.
Are you surprised by the soldier's actions?
What do you think he feels (*a*) about his own behaviour? (*b*) about the girl's situation?

▷ How do you feel about the girl and about the soldier at the end of the episode?

Reread the poem right through now to see what else deserves attention before choosing an assignment.

Assignments

English

○ *The Girl from the Guesthouse*
Rewrite this episode (in verse or prose) from the young soldier's point of view. Build upon the descriptive and narrative details that Lawrence gives us but add details of your own to bring out the soldier's mixed feelings – both about the horse and about the girl – as well as painting a picture of her.
Do you ever intend to return?

○ *Do You Understand?*
Two days after this episode, a letter arrives at the guesthouse for the girl. It is from the young soldier. Write that letter.

English Literature

○ Essay: 'The Soldier and his Mistress'.
What picture of the girl and of the young soldier is created here?
How does the episode which gives the poem its title suggest the soldier's attitude to life in general?
Do you have sympathy for the girl and/or the soldier?

○ Here is a poem written recently by a teenager.
How convincingly do you think it explores its speaker's circumstances and feelings?
What impression does it give you of the boy and the girl?
Which details do you think are most effective?
You may like to compare and contrast it with Lawrence's poem.

The Seduction

(A clumsy poem of teenage angst!!!)

After the party, early Sunday morning,
He led her to the quiet bricks of Birkenhead docks.
Far past the silver stream of traffic through the city,
Far from the blind windows of the tower blocks.

He sat down in the darkness, leather jacket creaking madly,   5
He spat into the river, fumbled in a bag.
He handed her the vodka, and she knocked it back like water,
She giggled, drunk and nervous, and he muttered 'little slag'.

She had met him at the party, and he'd danced with her all
                                        night.
He'd told her about football; Sammy Lee and Ian Rush.   10
She had nodded, quite enchanted, and her eyes were wide and
                                        bright
As he enthused about the Milk Cup, and the next McGuigan
                                        fight.

As he brought her more drinks, so she fell in love
With his eyes as blue as iodine,
With the fingers that stroked her neck and thighs   15
And the kisses that tasted of nicotine.

Then: 'I'll take you to the river where I spend the afternoons,
When I should be at school, or eating me dinner.
Where I go, by meself, with me dad's magazines
And a bag filled with shimmering, sweet paint thinner.'   20

So she followed him there, all high white shoes,
All wide blue eyes, and bottles of vodka.
And sat in the dark, her head rolling forward
Towards the frightening scum on the water.

And talked about school, in a disjointed way: 25
About O levels she'd be sitting in June
She chattered on, and stared at the water,
The Mersey, green as a septic wound.

Then, when he swiftly contrived to kiss her
His kiss was scented by Listerine   30
And she stifled a giggle, reminded of numerous
Stories from teenage magazines . . .

                         *

When she discovered she was three months gone
She sobbed in the cool, locked darkness of her room
And she ripped up all her *My Guy* and her *Jackie* photo-comics   35
Until they were just bright paper, like confetti, strewn
On the carpet. And on that day, she broke the heels
Of her high white shoes (as she flung them at the wall).
And realized, for once, that she was truly truly frightened
But more than that, cheated by the promise of it all.   40

For where, now, was the summer of her sixteenth year?
Full of glitzy fashion features, and stories of romance?
Where a stranger could lead you to bright new worlds,
And how would you know, if you never took a chance?

Full of glossy horoscopes, and glamour with a stammer;   45
Full of fresh fruit diets – how did she feel betrayed?
Now, with a softly rounded belly, she was sickened every
                                        morning
By stupid stupid promises, only tacitly made.

Where were the glossy photographs of summer,
Day trips to Blackpool, jumping all the rides?   50
And where, now, were the pink smiling faces in the picture:
Three girls paddling in the grey and frothy tide?

So she cried that she had missed all the innocence around her
And all the parties where you meet the boy next door,
Where you walk hand in hand, in an acne'd wonderland,   55
With a glass of lager-shandy, on a carpeted floor.

But, then again, better to be smoking scented drugs
Or festering, invisibly, unemployed.
Better to destroy your life in modern, man-made ways
Than to fall into this despicable, feminine void.   60

Better to starve yourself, like a sick, precocious child
Than to walk through town with a belly huge and ripe.
And better, now, to turn away, move away, fade away,
Than to have the neighbours whisper that 'you always looked
                                        the type'.

Eileen McAuley

☆

Further reading

Lawrence   Short stories   *The Prussian Officer*
                                     The Thorn in the Flesh
                                     The Mortal Coil

★

═ *Tennyson* ═
MARIANA

'there at the moated grange resides this dejected Mariana'

Tennyson took the idea for this poem from a single line of Shakespeare's *Measure for Measure*.
Mariana was engaged to Angelo who jilted her when the ship carrying her dowry was lost at sea.
Now, still pining for Angelo, she lives in lonely seclusion in a country house . . .

Read through the poem carefully two or three times before thinking about the points which follow.

Mariana

With blackest moss the flower-plots
   Were thickly crusted, one and all:
The rusted nails fell from the knots
   That held the pear to the garden-wall.
The broken sheds look'd sad and strange: 5
   Unlifted was the clinking latch;
   Weeded and worn the ancient thatch
Upon the lonely moated grange.
     She only said, 'My life is dreary,
       He cometh not,' she said;   10
     She said, 'I am aweary, aweary,
       I would that I were dead!'

Her tears fell with the dews at even;
   Her tears fell ere the dews were dried;
She could not look on the sweet heaven,   15
   Either at morn or eventide.
After the flitting of the bats,
   When thickest dark did trance the sky,
   She drew her casement-curtain by,
And glanced athwart the glooming flats.   20
     She only said, 'The night is dreary,
       He cometh not,' she said;
     She said, 'I am aweary, aweary,
       I would that I were dead!'

Upon the middle of the night,   25
   Waking she heard the night-fowl crow:
The cock sung out an hour ere light:
   From the dark fen the oxen's low
Came to her: without hope of change,

moated grange a country house surrounded by a water-filled ditch.

even, eventide evening.

morn morning.

trance put into a trance, a state between sleeping and waking.
casement window.
athwart across, from one side to the other.
glooming flats darkening, bleak flat countryside.

night-fowl night birds.
ere before.
fen low-lying marshland.
low sound made by cattle.

In sleep she seem'd to walk forlorn,   30   **forlorn** *deserted, neglected,*
Till cold winds woke the gray-eyed morn   *wretched.*
About the lonely moated grange.
    She only said, 'The day is dreary,
      He cometh not,' she said;
    She said, 'I am aweary, aweary,   35
      I would that I were dead!'

About a stone-cast from the wall   **stone-cast** *stone's throw.*
    A sluice with blacken'd waters slept,   **sluice** *flood gate.*
And o'er it many, round and small,
    The cluster'd marish-mosses crept.   40   **marish-mosses** *marsh-*
Hard by a poplar shook alway,   *mosses.*
                                                    poplar *a large, slender tree,*
    All silver-green with gnarlèd bark: *with quivering leaves.*
For leagues no other tree did mark   **gnarlèd** *rugged, weather-*
                                                    beaten.
The level waste, the rounding gray.   **leagues** *many miles.*
    She only said, 'My life is dreary,   45   **waste** *empty space.*
      He cometh not,' she said: **rounding** *surrounding.*
    She said, 'I am aweary, aweary,
      I would that I were dead!'

And ever when the moon was low,
    And the shrill winds were up and away, 50
In the white curtain, to and fro,
    She saw the gusty shadow sway.
But when the moon was very low,
    And wild winds bound within their cell,
    The shadow of the poplar fell   55
Upon her bed, across her brow.   **brow** *forehead.*
    She only said, 'The night is dreary,
      He cometh not,' she said:
    She said, 'I am aweary, aweary,
      I would that I were dead!'   60

All day within the dreamy house,
    The doors upon their hinges creak'd;
The blue fly sung in the pane; the mouse
    Behind the mouldering wainscot shriek'd,   **wainscot** *wooden*
Or from the crevice peer'd about.   65   *panelling.*
    Old faces glimmer'd thro' the doors,
    Old footsteps trod the upper floors,
Old voices called her from without.   **without** *outside.*
    She only said, 'My life is dreary,
      He cometh not,' she said;   70
    She said, 'I am aweary, aweary,
      I would that I were dead!'

The sparrow's chirrup on the roof,
    The slow clock ticking, and the sound
Which to the wooing wind aloof   75   **aloof** *proud, haughty.*
    The poplar made, did all confound   **confound her sense**
                                                    confuse and dismay her.

50

Her sense; but most she loathed the hour
   When the thick-moted sunbeam lay
   Athwart the chambers, and the day
Was sloping toward his western bower.
    Then, said she, 'I am very dreary,
      He will not come,' she said;
    She wept, 'I am aweary, aweary,
      O God, that I were dead!'

thick-moted picking up the
dust in the air.
chambers rooms.
80 *bower* shady resting place.

☆

Thinking/Talking Points

▷ How many words in the poem can you find whose sound is like someone grieving, weeping, moaning, lamenting?
Where does the poet imitate the rhythm of Mariana's sobbing?

▷ Which details in the description of the house and the countryside surrounding it reflect Mariana's feelings?

▷ How would you describe the mood created in the opening stanza?
What do these descriptive details contribute to that mood:
'blackest . . . rusted nails fell from . . . broken sheds . . . weeded and worn'?
How does this phrase make its effect:
'Unlifted was the clinking latch'?

▷ Reread stanzas 4 and 5.
How would you describe the mood here?
What connection is the poet implying between the sluice, the poplar and the girl?

▷ Look again at stanza 6.
What impression do these lines give you of the house?

▷ How does the final stanza make you feel about Mariana's situation?

▷ What sort of poem do you think Tennyson set out to write? (e.g. Is it a poem with a moral or political message? Does it examine Mariana's character and feelings? Do we enjoy it mostly for the story it tells, for the mood it generates, for the picturesque details, or because it sounds beautiful?)

Before you read the poem again, think which details of *Mariana* have already fixed themselves in your memory.

Assignments

English

○ *Alone and Far Away*
Create a similiar piece in verse or prose about a castaway on a cold, windswept, deserted island or about a prisoner in a lonely tower or deep, dark dungeon.
Decide if you will narrate the story as Tennyson does *Mariana*, or describe the situation through the castaway's/prisoner's eyes.

You do not need to explain *how* the person came to be in that situation: concentrate on giving the reader a strong sense of the place and of the captive's mood.

This is an exercise for which a thesaurus would be a useful tool.

○ See if you can develop one of these snatches from Shakespeare into a piece like *Mariana*:

'This will last out a night in Russia,
When nights are longest there.'

'In the East my pleasure lies.'

                    'But that I am forbid
To tell the secrets of my prison-house
I could a tale unfold whose lightest word
Would harrow up thy soul, freeze thy young blood . . .'

'We have heard the chimes at midnight.'

'The natural bravery of your isle, which stands
As Neptune's park, ribbed and paled in
With rocks unscalable, and roaring waters.'

'The west yet glimmers with some streaks of day:
Now spurs the lated traveller apace
To gain the timely inn.'

'The poor soul sat sighing by a sycamore tree.'

'Alack! the night comes on, and the bleak winds
Do sorely ruffle; for many miles about
There's scarce a bush . . . come out of the storm.'

'. . . old December's bareness everywhere.'

○ Make some illustrations for *Mariana of the Moated Grange*.

English Literature

○ Essay: With close attention to the text, examine the way the poet exploits various techniques to create the picture and mood of *Mariana*.
Why do you think the poem has been popular?
What is your own assessment of it?

★

═══ *Marvell* ═══
TO HIS COY MISTRESS

If Time had a face, what do you think it would look like?
If Time was a worker, what work would he/she do?
If you could ask Time a question, what would it be?
If you could ask Time a favour, what would that be?

If you could look through the photograph album of your life, what pictures, taken over the next fifty years, would you like to see recording the way you spent your time?

Read through the following poem carefully two or three times before considering the points which follow.

To His Coy Mistress

Had we but World enough, and Time,
This coyness Lady were no crime.
We would sit down, and think which way
To walk, and pass our long Loves Day.
Thou by the *Indian Ganges* side   5
Should'st Rubies find: I by the Tide
Of *Humber* would complain. I would
Love you ten years before the Flood:
And you should if you please refuse
Till the Conversion of the *Jews*.   10
My vegetable Love should grow
Vaster than Empires, and more slow.
An hundred years should go to praise
Thine Eyes, and on thy Forehead Gaze.
Two hundred to adore each Breast: 15
But thirty thousand to the rest.
An Age at least to every part,
And the last Age should show your Heart.
For Lady you deserve this State;
Nor would I love at lower rate.   20
   But at my back I alwaies hear
Times wingèd Charriot hurrying near:
And yonder all before us lye
Desarts of vast Eternity.
Thy Beauty shall no more be found;   25
Nor, in thy marble Vault, shall sound
My ecchoing Song: then Worms shall try
That long preserv'd Virginity:

mistress girlfriend.

Indian Ganges the mighty, splendid, sacred Indian river.
Humber by comparison, a dreary, unspectacular river, passing by Hull.
complain lament that my love was not returned.
the Flood Noah's Flood, one of the earliest events in human history.
the conversion of the Jews their conversion to Christianity was something predicted to occur just before the Day of Judgement.
vegetable growing very slowly but massively, like a tree.
an age a very long period of time.

wingèd flying.
yonder there, almost within sight.

marble vault tomb.
try probe, test, punish.

And your quaint Honour turn to dust;
And into ashes all my lust.   30
The Grave's a fine and private place,
But none I think do there embrace.
   Now therefore, while the youthful hew
Sits on thy skin like morning dew,
And while thy willing Soul transpires   35
At every pore with instant Fires,
Now let us sport us while we may;
And now, like am'rous birds of prey,
Rather at once our Time devour,
Than languish in his slow-chapt pow'r.   40
Let us roll all our Strength, and all
Our sweetness, up into one Ball:
And tear our Pleasures with rough strife,
Thorough the Iron gates of Life.
Thus, though we cannot make our Sun   45
Stand still, yet we will make him run.

quaint *prim, old-fashioned.*

youthful hew *the lovely, delicate complexion of a young girl.*
transpires *breathes out.*

sport us *enjoy ourselves.*
am'rous *ardent, passionate.*

languish *waste away.*
slow-chapt *with slowly grinding jaws.*

strife *struggling (with each other as they make love and against Time).*

☆

Thinking/Talking Points

▷   What other words and phrases could you use to describe a girl who was 'coy'?
Suggest a few reasons why a girl might be reluctant to respond to a boy who said he loved her.

▷   How would you describe the mood and tone of voice in the first paragraph?
How does the *sound* of the words and the length of the lines help to generate that mood?
What do you notice about the *way* the speaker addresses his girlfriend?
How is he trying to make her feel?

▷   Which word suddenly changes the mood of the poem?

▷   What tone of voice do you hear in the second paragraph?
How do you imagine 'Time's wingèd charriot'?
What does the speaker see coming after death?
How does the picture he paints of what will happen to his Lady affect you?

▷   Notice how the word 'Now' (line 33) again shifts the mood of the poem.
How many more times is the word used in this paragraph?
What tone of voice do you hear now?
What image of Time does this phrase conjure up:
'his slow-chapt pow'r'?
How does the speaker propose he and his lady outwit Time?
What contrasting aspects of love making are suggested by the phrase 'like am'rous birds of prey'?
What pictures do you see here:
'Let us roll all our Strength, and all
Our sweetness, up into one Ball'?

▷   How would you describe the mood of the final four lines of the poem?

Reread the poem now a couple of times to see what else deserves attention before you choose an assignment.

Assignments

English

○   Compose the coy mistress's reply, in verse or prose.

○   Write a dialogue between a modern couple: he is eager to settle down, get married, have children; she wants to pursue her career, travel, explore other relationships . . .

○   Make a drawing of Time suggested by the poem.

English Literature

○   Essay: With close attention to the text, examine the ways in which the speaker attempts to overcome the girl's coyness. Do you think he succeeds?

○   'The poem is as much a meditation on the shortness and joys of human life as a slick attempt to seduce.' Do you agree?
Refer closely to the text in your answer.

Some other poems on the theme of Mutability

Shakespeare   Sonnets (especially nos. 1–19; 60 [see page 162]; 64–65; 77; 81; 104; 123–124).
Shelley   *Ozymandias*

★

The Definition of Love

Is there a difference between love and friendship?
And between love and desire?

What would you list as the ingredients of true love?
Here are some things which one group suggested: trust; fun; mutual respect;
sex; money; class; comfort; security; excitement; passion; stability; people's
approval; intelligence; commitment; religion; mystery; pride; chastity; give
and take; food; health; devotion; age; children; fashion.
What would you add to/delete from the list?

Read through the following poem a few times and then consider the points
which follow. Do not worry if some of the language is unfamiliar to you.

The Good Morrow

I wonder by my troth, what thou, and I
Did, till we lov'd? were we not wean'd till then?
But suck'd on countrey pleasures, childishly?
Or snorted we i' the seaven sleepers den?
'Twas so; But this, all pleasures fancies bee.   5
If ever any beauty I did see,
Which I desir'd, and got, 'twas but a dreame of thee.

And now good morrow to our waking soules,
Which watch not one another out of feare;
For love, all love of other sights controules,   10
And makes one little roome, an every where.
Let sea-discoverers to new worlds have gone,
Let Maps to others, worlds or worlds have showne,
Let us possesse one world, each hath one, and is one.

My face in thine eyes, thine in mine appeares,   15
And true plaine hearts doe in the faces rest,
Where can we finde two better hemispheares
Without sharpe North, without declining West?
What ever dyes, was not mixt equally;
If our two loves be one, or, thou and I   20
Love so alike, that none doe slacken, none can die.

by my troth sincerely.

snorted . . . in the seaven sleepers den snored like the seven Ephesians who fell asleep in a cave and didn't wake up for 230 years.
but a dreame of thee just a pale imitation of you.
good morrow good morning, welcome.
feare distrust.

let . . . let's acknowledge that.

hemispheares half worlds.
sharpe cold, cruel.
mixt equally properly mixed.

none doe slacken if neither of us loves the other any less than we do now.

☆

Thinking/Talking Points

▷ What tone of voice do you hear in the opening lines of the poem? And at the end?

▷ Which words and phrases in the poem emphasise that the love the couple feels is mutual?
Do you feel that the man and the woman are equals here?

▷ What is the speaker saying in the first stanza about the couple's previous love affairs?

▷ See if you can express this bit in your own words:
'But this, all pleasures fancies bee'
(Try substituting the word 'are' for 'bee' and changing the order of the words.)

▷ Look again at stanza 2.
Why *do* the lovers watch one another?

▷ What do you think the speaker means when he says that 'love . . . makes one little roome, an every where'?

▷ Why isn't the speaker envious of those who've explored the world or made maps of previously unknown countries?
Why does the speaker feel the world made by the lovers is better than the world outside?
What will ensure that the couple's love will last forever?

▷ Which of your 'ingredients of true love' are apparent in this couple's relationship?

Read through the poem a couple more times now to see which other details deserve attention before choosing your assignment.

Assignments

English

○ Write a paragraph or a poem exploring the early morning thoughts of a boy or a girl who has just fallen in love.

○ Write a family conversation between a boy or girl of your age and his or her parents following the announcement that he or she intends to get married. Try to bring out their different ideas of what love and marriage entail.

○ Write a description of the sort of person you'd like to marry.
Are there things about yourself which may have to change before you can build a lasting relationship?

English Literature

○ What does Donne's poem tell us about the joys of and ingredients of true love? Remember to refer closely to the text in your answer.

○ Compare and contrast *The Good Morrow* with this sonnet by Shakespeare.

Sonnet 116

Let me not to the marriage of true minds
Admit impediments; love is not love
Which alters when it alteration finds,
Or bends with the remover to remove.
O, no, it is an ever-fixèd mark   5
That looks on tempests and is never shaken;
It is the star to every wand'ring bark,
Whose worth's unknown, although his height be taken.
Love's not Time's fool, though rosy lips and cheeks
Within his bending sickle's compass come;   10
Love alters not with his brief hours and weeks,
But bears it out even to the edge of doom.
If this be error and upon me proved,
I never writ, nor no man ever loved.

true faithful.

admit impediments
recognise, or allow any obstacles or objections.

the star to every wand'ring bark like a marker for ships at sea.
whose worth's unknown, although his height be taken *men navigate by the Pole Star even though they couldn't state its 'value'.*
fool *lackey, servant.*
within his bending sickle's compass come *are subject to/razed by Time's scythe.*
doom *the end of the world.*

Further reading

Donne   *The Sunne Rising*
Shakespeare   *Romeo and Juliet* Act I sc.v ll.46–146; Act II sc.ii; Act III sc.v.

★

Browning

from CHILDE ROLAND TO THE DARK TOWER CAME

This poem dramatises an episode from one of the legends of King Arthur and his Knights of the Round Table.

Roland is on a quest (a search) in which many others have failed. He must find the Dark Tower, Chapel Perilous. The Chapel is the resting place of the Holy Grail – the chalice which (according to legends) was used by Christ at the Last Supper and in which His blood was received from the Cross. The Grail was brought to Britain by Joseph of Arimathea and hidden in the Chapel.

Recovery of the Grail will restore health and fertility to a land under a curse. The kingdom has become a wasteland, a desert where nothing will grow. The young knight must pass through nightmarish countryside if he's to prove himself worthy of success. Browning's poem conjures up that wild landscape. (The word 'Childe' means something like 'a young, untried, apprentice knight'.)

Childe Roland to the Dark Tower Came

My first thought was, he lied in every word,
  That hoary cripple, with malicious eye
  Askance to watch the working of his lie
On mine, and mouth scarce able to afford
Suppression of the glee, that pursed and scored   5
  Its edge, at one more victim gained thereby.

What else should he be set for, with his staff?
  What, save to waylay with his lies, ensnare
  All travellers who might find him posted there,
And ask the road? I guessed what skull-like laugh   10
Would break, what crutch 'gin write my epitaph
  For pastime in the dusty thoroughfare,

If at his counsel I should turn aside
  Into that ominous tract which, all agree
  Hides the Dark Tower. Yet acquiescingly   15
I did turn as he pointed: neither pride
Nor hope rekindling at the end descried,
  So much as gladness that some end might be . . .

hoary grey with old age.
malicious having evil wishes, cruel.
askance squinting sideways, with mistrust.
glee delight.
pursed and scored screwed up, wrinkled.
waylay intercept, ambush.
ensnare trap.
posted on duty.
what crutch 'gin what crutch would begin to.
epitaph writing on a tombstone.
thoroughfare/tract road, path.
counsel advice.
ominous gloomy, threatening.
acquiescingly doing as he wished.
rekindling relighting, restoring.
descried imagined, seen far off.

60

So, quiet as despair, I turned from him,
    That hateful cripple, out of his highway   20
    Into the path he pointed. All the day
Had been a dreary one at best, and dim
Was settling to its close, yet shot one grim
    Red leer to see the plain catch its estray.

For mark! no sooner was I fairly found   25
    Pledged to the plain, after a pace or two,
    Than, pausing to throw backward a last view
O'er the safe road, 'twas gone; grey plain all round:
Nothing but plain to the horizon's bound.
    I might go on; nought else remained to do.   30

So, on I went. I think I never saw
    Such starved ignoble nature; nothing throve:
    For flowers – as well expect a cedar grove!
But cockle, spurge, according to their law
Might propagate their kind, with none to awe,   35
    You'd think; a burr had been a treasure-trove.

No! penury, inertness and grimace,
    In some strange sort, were the land's portion. 'See
    Or shut your eyes,' said Nature peevishly,
'It nothing skills: I cannot help my case: 40
'Tis the Last Judgment's fire must cure this place,
    Calcine its clods and set my prisoners free.'

If there pushed any ragged thistle-stalk
    Above its mates, the head was chopped; the bents
    Were jealous else. What made those holes and rents   45
In the dock's harsh swarth leaves, bruised as to baulk
All hope of greenness? 'tis a brute must walk
    Pashing their life out, with a brute's intents.

As for the grass, it grew as scant as hair
    In leprosy; thin dry blades pricked the mud   50
    Which underneath looked kneaded up with blood.
One stiff blind horse, his every bone a-stare,
Stood stupefied, however he came there:
    Thrust out past service from the devil's stud!

Alive? he might be dead for aught I know   55
    With that red gaunt and colloped neck a-strain,
    And shut eyes underneath the rusty mane;
Seldom went such grotesqueness with such woe;
I never saw a brute I hated so;
    He must be wicked to deserve such pain . . .   60

leer *wicked grin.*
estray *someone who has strayed into a trap.*

pledged *committed to.*

bound *limit, edge.*

ignoble *wretched, rough.*
throve *grew, flourished.*

cockle, spurge *weeds.*
propagate their kind *reproduce, flourish.*
awe *be surprised.*
burr *a rough, sticky plant.*
penury *utter poverty.*
inertness *stillness, paralysis.*
grimace *scowl, ugly expression.*
peevishly *irritably.*
'It nothing skills' *'There's nothing I can do about it'.*
calcine *burn to ashes.*
clods *lumps of earth.*
bents *coarse stiff grasses.*
rents *tears.*
dock *a large-leaved weed.*
swarth *dark.*
baulk *prevent.*
pashing *crushing.*
intents *intentions.*

leprosy *disfiguring and contagious disease.*
kneaded up *pounded like dough.*

stud *farm where horses are bred.*

colloped *cut, slashed or marked with ridges.*

61

A sudden little river crossed my path
    As unexpected as a serpent comes.
    No sluggish tide congenial to the glooms;
This, as it frothed by, might have been a bath
For the fiend's glowing hoof – to see the wrath   65
    Of its black eddy bespate with flakes and spumes.

So petty yet so spiteful! All along,
    Low scrubby alders kneeled down over it;
    Drenched willows flung them headlong in a fit
Of mute despair, a suicidal throng: 70
The river which had done them all the wrong,
    Whate'er that was, rolled by, deterred no whit.

Which, while I forded, – good saints, how I feared
    To set my foot upon a dead man's cheek
    Each step, or feel the spear I thrust to seek   75
For hollows, tangled in his hair or beard!
    – It may have been a water-rat I speared,
    But, ugh! it sounded like a baby's shriek.

Glad was I when I reached the other bank.
    Now for a better country. Vain presage!   80
    Who were the strugglers, what war did they wage
Whose savage trample thus could pad the dank
Soil to a plash? Toads in a poisoned tank,
    Or wild-cats in a red-hot iron cage –

The fight must so have seemed in that fell cirque.   85
    What penned them there, with all the plain to choose?
    No foot-print leading to that horrid mews,
None out of it. Mad brewage set to work
Their brains, no doubt, like galley-slaves the Turk
    Pits for his pastime, Christians against Jews.   90

And more than that – a furlong on – why, there!
    What bad use was that engine for, that wheel,
    Or brake, not wheel – that harrow fit to reel
Men's bodies out like silk? with all the air
Of Tophet's tool, on earth left unaware,   95
    Or brought to sharpen its rusty teeth of steel.

Then came a bit of stubbed ground, once a wood,
    Next a marsh, it would seem, and now mere earth
    Desperate and done with; (so a fool finds mirth,
Makes a thing and then mars it, till his mood   100
Changes and off he goes!) within a rood –
    Bog, clay and rubble, sand and stark black dearth.

tide current.
congenial fitting, appropriate.
wrath fury.
bespate spattered with.
spumes froth, foam.

deterred no whit not at all discouraged.

vain presage false hope.

pad walk carefully.
dank damp, decaying.
plash splash gently.

fell cirque terrible plain surrounded by hills, arena.

mews stable yard.

mad brewage drink which sends one mad.

pits sets against one another.
furlong one-eighth of a mile.
engine instrument of torture.

Tophet's tool Hell's instrument.

rood a quarter of an acre.

Now blotches rankling, coloured gay and grim,
   Now patches where some leanness of the soil's
   Broke into moss or substances like boils;   105
Then came some palsied oak, a cleft in him
Like a distorted mouth that splits its rim
   Gaping at death, and dies while it recoils.

And just as far as ever from the end!
   Nought in the distance but the evening, nought   110
   To point my footstep further! At the thought,
A great black bird, Apollyon's bosom-friend,
Sailed past, nor beat his wide wing dragon-penned
   That brushed my cap – perchance the guide I sought.

For, looking up, aware I somehow grew,   115
   'Spite of the dusk, the plain had given place
   All round to mountains – with such name to grace
Mere ugly heights and heaps now stolen in view.
How thus they had surprised me, – solve it, you!
   How to get from them was no clearer case.   120

Yet half I seemed to recognize some trick
   Of mischief happened to me, God knows when –
   In a bad dream perhaps. Here ended, then,
Progress this way. When, in the very nick
Of giving up, one time more, came a click   125
   As when a trap shuts – you're inside the den!

Burningly it came on me all at once,
   This was the place! those two hills on the right,
   Crouched like two bulls locked horn in horn in fight;
While to the left, a tall scalped mountain . . . Dunce,   130
Dotard, a-dozing at the very nonce,
   After a life spent training for the sight!

What in the midst lay but the Tower itself?
   The round squat turret, blind as the fool's heart,
   Built of brown stone, without a counterpart   135
In the whole world. The tempest's mocking elf
Points to the shipman thus the unseen shelf
   He strikes on, only when the timbers start.

Not see? because of night perhaps? – why, day
   Came back again for that! before it left,   140
   The dying sunset kindled through a cleft:
The hills, like giants at a hunting, lay,
Chin upon hand, to see the game at bay, –
   'Now stab and end the creature – to the heft!'

blotches rankling ugly
marks like festering ulcers.

palsied twisted, paralysed.
cleft split.

Apollyon's bosom-friend
Satan's accomplice.
dragon-penned with
wings like a dragon's.
perchance perhaps.

dotard imbecile.
nonce moment.

shelf sandbank.
start start to tear apart.

heft sword handle.

Not hear? when noise was everywhere! it tolled   145
    Increasing like a bell. Names in my ears,
    Of all the lost adventures my peers, –   *peers* fellow knights.
How such a one was strong, and such was bold,
And such was fortunate, yet each of old
    Lost, lost! one moment knelled the woe of years.   150   **knelled** rang the funeral
                                                                    bell.

There they stood, ranged along the hill-sides, met
    To view the last of me, a living frame
    For one more picture! in a sheet of flame
I saw them and I knew them all. And yet
Dauntless the slug-horn to my lips I set,   155   **dauntless** boldly, bravely.
    And blew *Childe Roland to the Dark Tower came.*   **slug-horn** a trumpet,
                                                                    probably here the word
                                                                    means a bugle made of
                                                                    ox-horn.

Thinking/Talking Points

▷   Which details in the description of the old man do you find chilling?
    Why do you think Roland decides to follow the old man's directions despite his
    suspicions?
    How do you imagine he feels as he turns into 'that ominous tract'?

▷   What is the first mysterious thing to happen to the young knight?
    How does that make the journey ahead seem particularly perilous?

▷   Look again at lines 31–51.
    What do you think Roland means when he says 'a burr had been a treasure-
    trove'?
    Which details make the place feel dangerous as well as bleak?

▷   What do you feel as you read the description of the horse (lines 52–60)?

▷   Look again at lines 61–78.
    'So petty yet so spiteful!'
    How does the poet make the river seem spiteful?

▷   Look again at lines 79–108.
    Can you describe in your own words what the knight found across the river?

▷   Now read through the rest of the poem again.
    How does the appearance of the bird at first suggest terror, then hope?
    Can you explain what has happened to the landscape?
    Why do you think the knight was at first unable to see the Chapel or to hear
    the bells?
    What impressions are we given of the Chapel? Was it what you expected?
    What thoughts and feelings do you imagine passing through Roland as he
    sounds his slug-horn?

    Reread the poem now and make a note of the details which you find most
    dramatic before you choose an assignment.

Assignments

English

○ Beginning from the moment when you meet an old man on the road, invent your own nightmarish search for Chapel Perilous.
Write (in verse or prose) in the first person recording not only what you see and hear but also how you feel at different moments of the quest.

○ Continue the story from the point where the poem ends.
What does the Chapel contain? Is recovery of the Holy Grail straightforward or are there other kinds of test which Roland must pass through?
What happens when he takes the Grail in his hands?
You may like to see if you can continue in Browning's style; alternatively you may write in prose.

○ Produce some illustrations for Browning's poem.

English Literature

○ Essay: With close reference to the text, show how Browning helps us to share the terrors of Childe Roland's quest.

Suggestions for further work

English

○ You might like to look at other episodes from the legends of Arthur and his knights and adapt them into short stories, poems or plays of your own. There are many excellent versions available including the following:

Malory	*Le Morte d'Arthur* edited by Field (Hodder and Stoughton) There is a modernised version by Loomis and Willard (Appleton Century Crofts)
Lang	*King Arthur: Tales of the Round Table* (Faber)
Green	*King Arthur and his Knights of the Round Table* (Puffin)
Steinbeck	*The Acts of King Arthur and his Noble Knights* (Pan)
Fraser	*King Arthur and the Knights of the Round Table* (Sidgwick & Jackson)

English Literature

○ Compare Browning's poem with T. S. Eliot's version of the approach to the Chapel (*The Waste Land* 'What the Thunder Said' lines 331–394).
By referring closely to the texts, note the significant differences. Say which version you find the more dramatic and why.

★

═ *Shakespeare* ═
THE EVE OF AGINCOURT

25th October 1415.

It is the middle of the night before the Battle of Agincourt.
The English forces are massively outnumbered by the French. The two armies are camped within sight, within earshot of one another.

This is how Shakespeare sets the scene.

Chorus

Now entertain conjecture of a time
When creeping murmur and the poring dark
Fills the wide vessel of the universe.
From camp to camp through the foul womb of night
The hum of either army stilly sounds,   *5*
That the fix'd sentinels almost receive
The secret whispers of each other's watch:
Fire answers fire, and through their paly flames
Each battle sees the other's umber'd face.
Steed threatens steed, in high and boastful neighs   *10*
Piercing the night's dull ear; and from the tents
The armourers, accomplishing the knights,
With busy hammers closing rivets up,
Give dreadful note of preparation.
The country cocks do crow, the clocks do toll,   *15*
And the third hour of drowsy morning name.

Proud of their numbers and secure in soul,
The confident and over-lusty French
Do the low-rated English play at dice;
And chide the cripple tardy-gaited night   *20*
Who, like a foul and ugly witch, doth limp
So tediously away. The poor condemned English,
Like sacrifices, by their watchful fires
Sit patiently, and inly ruminate
The morning's danger, and their gesture sad   *25*
Investing lank-lean cheeks and war-worn coats
Presenteth them unto the gazing moon
So many horrid ghosts.

Glossary (margin notes):

entertain conjecture of *imagine.*

the wide vessel of the universe *all of heaven and earth.*

fix'd sentinels *soldiers on watch.*

umber'd *shadowy.*

steed *horse.*

accomplishing *equipping.*

toll *sound the hour.*

secure in soul *smug.*

over-lusty *too high-spirited.*

low-rated *regarded as having no chance of winning.*

chide *tell off.*

tardy-gaited *limping by too slowly.*

like sacrifices *looking as if they're about to be sacrificed to a god.*

inly ruminate *think to themselves about.*

investing lank-lean cheeks *showing itself in their hollow cheeks.*

O now, who will behold

The royal captain of this ruin'd band	30
Walking from watch to watch, from tent to tent,	
Let him cry, 'Praise and glory on his head!'	
For forth he goes and visits all his host,	
Bids them good-morrow with a modest smile,	
And calls them brothers, friends and countrymen.	35
Upon his royal face there is no note	
How dread an army had enrounded him;	
Nor doth he dedicate one jot of colour	
Unto the weary and all-watched night;	
But freshly looks and over-bears attaint	40
With cheerful semblance and sweet majesty;	
That every wretch, pining and pale before,	
Beholding him, plucks comfort from his looks.	
A largess universal like the sun	
His liberal eye doth give to every one,	45
Thawing cold fear, that mean and gentle all,	
Behold, as may unworthiness define,	
A little touch of Harry in the night.	

from *Henry V* Act IV sc.i

ruin'd band *ragged, demoralised army.*

good-morrow *good morning.*

enrounded *surrounded.*
dedicate *offer.*

over-bears attaint with cheerful semblance *puts on such a cheerful manner that no one would guess he was exhausted.*
beholding *seeing.*
a largess universal . . . every one *he is so kind that when he looks on his men it is as if the sun is showering them with blessings.*
mean and gentle all *both the common soldiers and their aristocratic generals.*
as may unworthiness define *if I, an unworthy poet, may express it so clumsily.*

Thinking/Talking Points

▷ What do we mean by 'poring over a book'?
How does the phrase 'the poring dark' make you feel?

▷ Which details capture the awful silence of the night?
Why is the sound of the armourers described as 'dreadful note of preparation'?
What feelings do you think might be passing through the minds of the young boys who looked after the horses and equipment in the English camp?

▷ Imagine you were trying to 'translate' this speech into film.
What would you show here:
'Fire answers fire, and through their paly flames
Each battle sees the other's umber'd face.'?

▷ What impression are we given of the French camp?
Can you suggest why the English are described as 'So many horrid ghosts'?

▷ What do you think the purpose of the English King's 'visits' was?
What impression of his personality are we given in this extract?
What difference in meaning is there between Shakespeare's phrase:
'A little touch of Harry in the night'
and this version:
'On the eve of battle, His Majesty, King Henry, toured the camp and talked to the common soldiers'?

68

Read through the passage again a couple of times now to see what other points need thinking about before you choose an assignment.

Assignments

English

○ Using some of the details from this Chorus but adding plenty of descriptive and reflective detail of your own, write, in the form of a letter home or as a diary entry, an account of this night as it might have been experienced by one of the boys.

○ Rewrite this passage, in verse or prose, to suit a play about modern warfare.

English Literature

○ With close attention to the text, discuss how these lines set the scene and convey to us the atmosphere on the eve of the great battle.

★

=== *Holub* ===
THE FLY

'I wish I'd been a fly on the wall.'
What do people mean when they say that?
How do you think a fly's eye would view what's going on around you at this moment?

The Fly

She sat on a willow-trunk
watching
part of the battle of Crécy,
the shouts,
the gasps,   5
the groans,
the tramping and the tumbling.

During the fourteenth charge
of the French cavalry
she mated   10
with a brown-eyed male fly
from Vadincourt.

She rubbed her legs together
as she sat on a disembowelled horse
meditating   15
on the immortality of flies.

With relief she alighted
on the blue tongue
of the Duke of Clervaux.

When silence settled   20
and only the whisper of decay
softly circled the bodies

and only
a few arms and legs
still twitched jerkily under the trees,   25

she began to lay her eggs
on the single eye
of Johann Uhr,
the Royal Armourer.

And thus it was   30
that she was eaten by a swift
fleeing
from the fires of Estrées.

battle of Crécy 26 August 1346. The first battle of the Hundred Years' War, in which the English heavily defeated the French.

disembowelled gutted.
meditating on thinking about.
immortality everlasting life.
alighted landed.

70   ☆

Thinking/Talking Points

▷ Why do you think
'the shouts,
the gasps
the groans'
are written as three separate, short lines?

▷ Look again at stanza 2.
What is the effect of describing two very different activities side by side?
Which seems to be the more important?

▷ Look again at the third stanza.
How would you describe the fly's outlook on life?
How is she punished for this later?

▷ How does stanza 4 make you feel?
Can you explain why?

▷ In what tone of voice would you read this:
'and only
a few arms and legs
still twitched jerkily under the trees'?
Which words capture the movements they describe?

▷ Do you think the poem has a serious point to make?
If so, what is it?

Read *The Fly* again now to see if any other points need thinking about before you choose an assignment.

Assignments

English

○ *Insect's Eye View*
Choose an insect and, in verse or prose, write an insect's eye view of one of the following occasions, bringing out how what is so very important to the people involved, is of only secondary interest to the insect:

a rugby match	a royal wedding
a pop concert	a lovers' meeting
a family rumpus	a maths lesson

English Literature

○ Essay: Referring closely to the text, show how, despite its flippant tone, *The Fly* is a serious and skilfully written poem.

○ Compare and contrast Holub's *The Fly* with Auden's poem *Musée des Beaux Arts*.

★

Owen

THE SEND-OFF

What sights and sounds, what atmosphere would you expect there to be on a railway station platform where families and friends were saying goodbye to sons and husbands going off to war?
Jot down a few phrases to describe the scene you imagine.

Read through the following poem two or three times before considering the points which follow.

The Send-Off

Down the close, darkening lanes they sang their way
To the siding-shed,
And lined the train with faces grimly gay.

Their breasts were stuck all white with wreath and spray
As men's are, dead.   5

Dull porters watched them, and a casual tramp
Stood staring hard,
Sorry to miss them from the upland camp.
Then, unmoved, signals nodded, and a lamp
Winked to the guard.   10

So secretly, like wrongs hushed-up, they went.
They were not ours:
We never heard to which front these were sent.

Nor there if they yet mock what women meant
Who gave them flowers.   15

Shall they return to beatings of great bells
In wild train-loads?
A few, a few, too few for drums and yells,
May creep back, silent, to still village wells
Up half-known roads.   20

☆

Thinking/Talking Points

▷   Suggest a few words and phrases of your own to describe this particular send-off.
Was the scene similar to the one you imagined before reading the poem?

▷   What pictures and feelings do these phrases suggest to you:
'the close, darkening lanes'
'they sang their way'
'grimly gay'

▷   How would you describe the behaviour of (a) the tramp (b) the signals, the lamp and the guard?

▷   Why will only 'a few' soldiers 'creep back, silent'?
Why will the roads be only 'half-known' to them?
In what tone of voice would you read the final stanza?

Read the poem again now before choosing your assignment.

Assignments

English

○   Imagine you are the mother or girlfriend of one of the soldiers.
Write two diary entries: (a) for the day he said goodbye, and (b) for the day he returned.
Use details from the poem but add plenty of your own ideas.
Try to convey your feelings on each occasion.

English Literature

○   Essay: 'What makes this poem so poignant and moving is that it works mainly by suggestion, by understatement rather than by telling us anything directly'.
Do you agree?
(Remember to refer closely to the text in your answer, showing how the poet uses a few significant details to create a mood of uneasiness.)

★

DULCE ET DECORUM EST

Scott of Amwell
THE DRUM

'It is a lovely and honourable thing, to die for one's country'

Horace 65–8 BC

What image(s) of the soldier are you most familiar with from magazines, television and films? See if you can recall a recent typical example.

Think about the way the following aspects of being a soldier are usually presented: uniform (picture the boots); drill; discipline; comradeship; physique; manliness; bravery; patriotism; glory; morale.

What image(s) does the slogan 'The Professionals' suggest to you?

Try to recall a particular war film you have seen.
What do you remember of any of the battle scenes?
Were the soldiers' behaviour and attitudes believable?
What feelings did the episodes stir in you?
What do you think the director's attitude to war was?

Do you think there is any harm in children playing at being soldiers?

Read through the following poem carefully two or three times before thinking about the points which follow.

Dulce et Decorum Est*

Bent double, like old beggars under sacks,
Knock-kneed, coughing like hags, we cursed through sludge,
Till on the haunting flares we turned our backs
And towards our distant rest began to trudge.
Men marched asleep. Many had lost their boots   5
But limped on, blood-shod. All went lame; all blind;
Drunk with fatigue; deaf even to the hoots
Of gas-shells dropping softly behind.

Gas! Gas! Quick, boys – An ecstasy of fumbling,
Fitting the clumsy helmets just in time;   10
But someone was still yelling out and stumbling
And flound'ring like a man in fire or lime . . .
Dim, through the misty panes and thick green light,
As under a green sea, I saw him drowning.

In all my dreams, before my helpless sight,   15
He plunges at me, guttering, choking, drowning.

hags ugly old women.

haunting flares the ghostly glow of magnesium flares fired to illuminate the battlefield.

fatigue exhaustion.

an ecstasy of fumbling a wild panic – all thumbs as they struggle with the gasmasks.

flound'ring struggling clumsily, helplessly.
lime quicklime, a chemical used to burn corpses.

plunges at lunges towards.
guttering spluttering out like a candle.

If in some smothering dreams you too could pace
Behind the wagon that we flung him in,
And watch the white eyes writhing in his face,
His hanging face, like a devil's sick of sin;   20
If you could hear, at every jolt, the blood
Come gargling from the froth-corrupted lungs,
Obscene as cancer, bitter as the cud
Of vile, incurable sores on innocent tongues, –
My friend, you would not tell with such high zest   25
To children ardent for some desperate glory,
The old Lie: *Dulce et decorum est*
Pro patria mori.

smothering suffocating.
pace walk.

writhing twisting in
agony.

froth-corrupted lungs the
effects of mustard-gas.
obscene disgusting.
cud chewed food.
zest enthusiasm.
ardent eager.

***Dulce et decorum est pro patria mori** a Latin motto which*
means 'It is lovely and honourable to die for your country'.

☆

Thinking/Talking Points

▷ What kind of poem did the title lead you to expect?
What impact did the opening line have on you?

▷ Which details in the first stanza mock the glamorised picture of war which is
often presented to the young?
Examine the way the *sounds* and *textures* of the key words in the stanza help to
make the scene vivid.

▷ What impression of the gas shells do these details give you: 'hoots . . . dropping
softly behind'?

▷ See if you can explain *how* the opening of stanza 2 captures the alarm as the
soldiers become aware of the cloud of gas trapping them.
What do you picture, how do you feel as you read
        'An ecstasy of fumbling,
Fitting the clumsy helmets just in time'?

▷ Look again at lines 11–16.
Which words capture the agony of the dying soldier?
Can you suggest why his death is like drowning?
How does the speaker share with us his own sense of helplessness?
How do you imagine his nightmares?

▷ What point do you think the poet is making when he tells us about 'the wagon
that we flung him in' (line 18)?
What is the effect on you of the way the corpse is described?

▷ Whom do you think the poet is addressing as 'My friend' (line 25)?
In what tone of voice do you think he says it?
In the light of what we've seen and heard, why is *Dulce et decorum est pro patria
mori* simply a lie?

Reread the poem to see what other details are worth attention before you
choose an assignment.

Assignments

English

○ *Initiation*
Use this poem as a starting point for an account of this episode in the form of a diary entry or a letter home written by a young recruit for whom this is the first experience of battle.
Try to make your own descriptive details as vivid as Owen's but concentrate on the young soldier's feelings as he compares what he is going through with the picture of soldiering which persuaded him to volunteer for the army.

○ Draw a series of cartoon pictures to illustrate this poem and to dramatise the points the poet is making.

○ *Join the Professionals*
See if you can write a contemporary version of Owen's poem.

English Literature

○ Essay: 'Died some, pro patria,
non "dulce" non "et decor" . . .
walked eye-deep in hell
believing in old men's lies . . .'   (Pound)
With close reference to the text, describe how Owen's poem challenges the glamorised picture of war often presented to the young.

○ Compare and contrast *Dulce et Decorum Est* with this earlier example of anti-war poetry:

The Drum

I hate that drum's discordant sound,	**discordant** *harsh, unmusical.*
Parading round, and round, and round:	
To thoughtless youth it pleasure yields,	
And lures from cities and from fields,	**lures** *tempts, beckons.*
To sell their liberty for charms 5	**liberty** *freedom.*
Of tawdry lace, and glittering arms;	**tawdry** *gaudy and worthless.*
And when Ambition's voice commands,	
To march, and fight, and fall, in foreign lands.	
I hate that drum's discordant sound,	
Parading round, and round, and round: 10	
To me it talks of ravaged plains,	**ravaged** *devastated.*
And burning towns, and ruined swains,	**swains** *young men.*
And mangled limbs, and dying groans,	
And widows' tears, and orphans' moans;	
And all that Misery's hand bestows, 15	
To fill the catalogue of human woes.	

John Scott of Amwell (1750–1783)

★

77

Yevtushenko
THE COMPANION

Read through the following poem two or three times. Then think about the points which follow.

The Companion

She was sitting on the rough embankment,
her cape too big for her tied on slapdash   **slapdash** *hastily,*
over an odd little hat with a bobble on it,   *carelessly.*
her eyes brimming with tears of hopelessness.
An occasional butterfly floated down   5
fluttering warm wings onto the rails.
The clinkers underfoot were deep lilac.   **clinkers** *ash and rubble*
We got cut off from our grandmothers   *over which railway lines are*
while the Germans were dive-bombing the train.   *laid.*
Katya was her name. She was nine.   10
I'd no idea what I could do about her,
but doubt quickly dissolved to certainty;
I'd have to take this thing under my wing;
– girls were in some sense of the word human,
a human being couldn't just be left.   15
The droning in the air and the explosions   **droning** *deep, monotonous*
receded farther into the distance,   *hum.*
I touched the little girl on her elbow.   **receded** *died away.*
'Come on. Do you hear? What are you waiting for?'
The world was big and we were not big,   20
and it was tough for us to walk across it.
She had galoshes on and felt boots,   **galoshes** *overshoes to keep*
I had a pair of second-hand boots.   *out the rain.*
We forded streams and tramped across the forest;   **forded** *waded across.*
each of my feet at every step it took   25
taking a smaller step inside the boot.
The child was feeble, I was certain of it.
'Boo-hoo,' she'd say. 'I'm tired,' she'd say.
She'd tire in no time I was certain of it,
but as things turned out it was me who tired.   30
I growled I wasn't going any further
and sat down suddenly beside the fence.
'What's the matter with you?' she said.
'Don't be so stupid! Put grass in your boots.
Do you want to eat something? Why won't you talk?   35
Hold this tin, this is crab.
We'll have refreshments. You small boys,

you're always pretending to be brave.'
Then out I went across the prickly stubble
marching beside her in a few minutes.   *40*
Masculine pride was muttering in my mind:
I scraped together strength and I held out
for fear of what she'd say. I even whistled.
Grass was sticking out from my tattered boots.
So on and on   *45*
we walked without thinking of rest
passing craters, passing fire,
under the rocking sky of '41
tottering crazy on its smoking columns.

craters holes in the ground made by shells or bombs.
'41 1941, the year Germany invaded Russia.
tottering unsteady, about to fall.

☆

Thinking/Talking Points

▷ How would you describe the mood of the opening lines?
   Which details do most to fix that mood?

▷ What is our first impression of the girl?
   From whose point of view are we seeing her?

▷ Which details gradually reveal the circumstances of this meeting?
   Why do you think the speaker says so little about what happened to the train?
   How do you imagine that scene?

▷ What do you think this means:
   'The world was big and we were not big'?

▷ How does the children's relationship gradually change?
   What do you think makes her stronger than he is?

▷ Look again at the last six lines of the poem.
   What thoughts do you imagine passing through the boy's mind?

   Read the poem again now before choosing an assignment.
   Think about which details make it dramatic.
   In what tone of voice would you read it aloud?

Assignments

English

○ Write a short story about this experience, from either child's point of view,
   adding to the details we are given. (Do not include too many events:
   concentrate upon description – e.g. of the terrain the children cross, of the
   destruction they see – and the thoughts/hopes/fears/questions which pass
   through the mind of the storyteller.) You may like to illustrate your work.

○ Rewrite the poem from the girl's point of view.

★

MORE LIGHT!
MORE LIGHT!

What is the most horrible death you can imagine?
Do you think your state of mind could ease (or make worse) the pain of a
violent, tortured death?
Would the attitude of those around you make any difference to how you felt?

In this disturbing poem, we are told about a martyr's hideous death and then
about an execution which is even more horrible.
The fact that these things really happened makes reading about them even
more difficult. You may prefer to turn the page and look at something less
distressing.

Read through the poem carefully two or three times and give yourself time to
think about why the poet may have decided to write it. Then consider the
points which follow.

More Light! More Light!*

For Heinrich Blücher and Hannah Arendt

Composed in the Tower before his execution
These moving verses, and being brought at that time
Painfully to the stake, submitted, declaring thus:
'I implore my God to witness that I have made no crime!'

Nor was he forsaken of courage, but the death was horrible,   5
The sack of gunpowder failing to ignite.
His legs were blistered sticks on which the black sap
Bubbled and burst as he howled for the Kindly Light.

And that was but one, and by no means one of the worst;
Permitted at least his pitiful dignity;   10
And such as were by made prayers in the name of Christ,
That shall judge all men, for his soul's tranquillity.

We move now to outside a German wood.
Three men are there commanded to dig a hole
In which the two Jews are ordered to lie down   15
And be buried alive by the third, who is a Pole.

Not light from the shrine at Weimar beyond the hill
Nor light from heaven appeared. But he did refuse.
A Lüger settled back deeply in its glove.
He was ordered to change places with the Jews.   20

the Tower *the tower of London.*
the stake *the post to which people sentenced to be burnt alive (e.g. for heresy) were tied.*
submitted *surrendered.*
implore *beg.*
the sack of gunpowder *thrown into the fire to cut short the martyr's suffering.*
the Kindly Light *God's love, grace, mercy.*

permitted *allowed.*

tranquillity *peace.*

Lüger *a pistol.*

80

Much casual death had drained away their souls.
The thick dirt mounted toward the quivering chin.
When only the head was exposed the order came
To dig him out again and to get back in.

No light, no light in the blue Polish eye.   *25*
When he finished a riding boot packed down the earth.
The Lüger hovered lightly in its glove.
He was shot in the belly and in three hours bled to death.

No prayers or incense rose up in those hours   **incense** *fragrant smoke*
Which grew to be years, and every day came mute   *30*   *used in church ceremonies.*
Thousands sifting down through the crisp air   **mute** *silent.*
And settled upon his eyes in a black soot.

** **More light!** supposedly the dying words of the German poet, Goethe, buried*
at Weimar. Goethe stood for 'the Good Germany' and hated the Prussians'
blind patriotism and their enthusiasm for all things military.

Thinking/Talking Points

▷   How did you feel as you read stanza 4?
    Why do you think it is written so bluntly?

▷   What foreknowledge on the reader's part is the poet counting on?
    What pictures do the words 'German . . . Jews' immediately throw up in your
    mind?
    How did you expect the poem to end?

▷   The Pole saw 'no light' to inspire him 'But he did refuse'.
    Why do you think he refused?
    Do you think you would have acted as he did?

▷   Why do you think the two Jews obeyed the command?
    Which detail captures the Pole's terror?

▷   Can you offer any explanation of why the German officer acted so barbarically?
    What do you think was passing through his mind as he walked away?

▷   See if you can work out what horrors are being described in the final stanza.
    Can you account for those lines seeming less disturbing than what has gone
    before, despite the scale of the atrocity they recall?

▷   The poem began with an account of another gruesome episode, hundreds of
    years earlier.
    What point(s) do you think the poet was making by putting these two episodes
    side by side (e.g. Have the two 'executions' much in common? Do you feel one
    is in any way less atrocious than the other?)

    Reread the poem to see what else needs thinking about before you choose your
    assignment.

Assignments

English

o   *The Onlooker*
You are the German officer's orderly who stands by and watches and does nothing to interfere.
Describe and explain your feelings (a) in a letter home or diary entry, or (b) in a story, written in the first person.

o   *Judgement Day*
Write a short play in which the officer and his orderly are on trial for War Crimes.
What excuse does each make for his behaviour?
What is the attitude of the judge, of the families of the victims, of the newspaper and television reporters to what happened so many years ago?

English Literature

o   *Time to Forgive and Forget?*
What do you suppose Hecht's purpose was in writing this poem?
Is its ugliness justified by its purpose?
Do you feel that you understand the people who continue to hunt for war criminals better now than you did before?
Do you think it's time there was an amnesty for such people?

Further reading

Primo Levi   *If This Is A Man*
Tadeusz Borowski   *This Way For The Gas, Ladies And Gentlemen*

★

What do you understand by the word 'progress'?

Do you think we live in a progressive society?
What do you think makes life today better than it was a hundred years ago?
(e.g. votes for women? the invention of television, of nuclear energy, of the
microchip? the abolition of capital punishment? health care and education for
all?)

Make your own list of major discoveries, inventions and improvements in the
way we live, which have come about over the last century.
Does anything on your list have unwelcome side-effects?

Do you think that there are any ways in which life today is worse than it was
one hundred years ago?

Read through the following poem carefully two or three times before looking
at the points which follow.

The Horses

Barely a twelvemonth after
The seven days war that put the world to sleep,
Late in the evening the strange horses came.
By then we had made our covenant with silence,   *covenant* pact, contract.
But in the first few days it was so still   5
We listened to our breathing and were afraid.
On the second day
The radios failed; we turned the knobs; no answer.
On the third day a warship passed us, heading north,
Dead bodies piled on the deck. On the sixth day   10
A plane plunged over us into the sea. Thereafter
Nothing. The radios dumb;
And still they stand in corners of our kitchens,
And stand, perhaps, turned on, in a million rooms
All over the world. But now if they should speak,   15
If on a sudden they should speak again,
If on the stroke of noon a voice should speak,
We would not listen, we would not let it bring
That old bad world that swallowed its children quick
At one great gulp. We would not have it again.   20
Sometimes we think of the nations lying asleep,
Curled blindly in impenetrable sorrow,   *impenetrable* impossible to break through.
And then the thought confounds us with its strangeness.   *confounds* confuses, bothers.
The tractors lie about our fields; at evening

They look like dank sea-monsters crouched and waiting. 25   **dank** *damp and*
We leave them where they are and let them rust: *unpleasant.*
'They'll moulder away and be like other loam.'
We make our oxen drag our rusty ploughs,   **moulder away** *deteriorate,*
Long laid aside. We have gone back   *decay.*
Far past our fathers' land. 30   **loam** *rich, fertile soil.*
                             And then, that evening
Late in the summer the strange horses came.
We heard a distant tapping on the road,
A deepening drumming; it stopped, went on again
And at the corner changed to hollow thunder. 35
We saw the heads
Like a wild wave charging and were afraid.
We had sold our horses in our fathers' time
To buy new tractors. Now they were strange to us
As fabulous steeds set on an ancient shield 40   **fabulous steeds** *horses in a*
Or illustrations in a book of knights.   *fairy story or a legend,*
We did not dare go near them. Yet they waited,   *wonderful.*
Stubborn and shy, as if they had been sent
By an old command to find our whereabouts
And that long-lost archaic companionship. 45   **archaic companionship**
In the first moment we had never a thought   *ancient, old-fashioned kind*
That they were creatures to be owned and used.   *of friendship.*
Among them were some half-a-dozen colts   **colts** *young horses.*
Dropped in some wilderness of the broken world,
Yet new as if they had come from their own Eden. 50   **Eden** *paradise.*
Since then they have pulled our ploughs and borne our loads   **borne** *carried.*
But that free servitude still can pierce our hearts.   **free servitude** *voluntary*
Our life is changed; their coming our beginning.   *service.*

☆

Thinking/Talking Points

▷   Which of these words do you think best describe(s) the mood of the speaker:
angry, calm, happy, resigned, anxious, confident, suspicious, secure, sorrowful,
relieved, upset, optimistic, cynical, energetic, alert, cool, agitated, relaxed, sad,
thoughtful, flippant, gloomy, wistful.

▷   When does this episode take place? Suggest where the poem might be set.

▷   How would you describe the atmosphere of 'the first few days'?
What do you imagine the survivors thinking and feeling?

▷   Which details emphasise that the people are cut off from the rest of the world?
Why do you think no one would listen even if the radios spoke?

▷   Look again at lines 18–20, 29–30 and 38–39.
Why do you think the speaker feels as he does about his father's generation?

▷   Why were the tractors left to rust?

▷ How does the poet create the sensation of the horses getting nearer?
What do you imagine the horses looked like?
Do you think you would have reacted to the horses in the same way as the people in the poem did?

▷ See if you can put the final line of the poem into your own words.

Read the poem again before choosing your assignment.

Assignments

English

○ Rewrite this poem as a series of diary entries, a few months apart. Begin immediately after the war. Use details from the poem but add plenty of your own descriptions and thoughts and feelings.

○ *Short Story* (own title)
Imagine a situation ten years after the arrival of the horses. The family hears an unfamiliar noise on the road and then catches sight of a huge truck rumbling up the drive. Who is in it? What happens?

English Literature

○ Essay: What do you think Edwin Muir is warning us about in *The Horses*?
Do you think it is a gloomy poem?
Remember to refer closely to the text in your answer.

Some other works which explore this theme:

Poems
James Kirkup	*No More Hiroshimas*
Peter Porter	*Your Attention Please*

Novels
Nevil Shute	*On The Beach*
Robert O'Brien	*Z for Zachariah*
John Christopher	*Empty World*
Swindells	*Brother in the Land*

Short story
Ray Bradbury	*There Will Come Soft Rains*

Films
Peter Watkins	*The War Game*
Barry Hines	*Threads*
Raymond Briggs	*When the Wind Blows*

Documentary
John Hersey	*Hiroshima*

★

Brooke
THE SOLDIER

McGough
WHY PATRIOTS ARE A BIT NUTS IN THE HEAD

Read through the following poems carefully two or three times before considering the points which follow.

The Soldier

If I should die, think only this of me:
    That there's some corner of a foreign field
That is for ever England. There shall be
    In that rich earth a richer dust concealed;
A dust whom England bore, shaped, made aware,   *5*
    Gave, once, her flowers to love, her ways to roam,
A body of England's, breathing English air,
    Washed by the rivers, blest by suns of home.

And think, this heart, all evil shed away,
    A pulse in the eternal mind, no less   *10*
    Gives somewhere back the thoughts by England given;
Her sights and sounds; dreams happy as her day;
    And laughter, learnt of friends; and gentleness,
    In hearts at peace, under an English heaven.

Why Patriots are a Bit Nuts in the Head

Patriots are a bit nuts in the head
because they wear
red, white and blue-
tinted spectacles
(red for blood   *5*
white for glory
and blue . . .
for a boy)
and are in effervescent danger

of losing their lives   *10*
lives are good for you
when you are alive
you can eat and drink a lot
and go out with girls
(sometimes if you are lucky   *15*
you can even go to bed with them)
but you can't do this
if you have your belly shot away
and your seeds
spread over some corner of a foreign field   *20*
to facilitate
in later years
the growing of oats by some peasant yobbo

when you are posthumous it is cold and dark
and that is why patriots are a bit nuts in the head

☆

Thinking/Talking Points

▷   Suggest likely dates for the composition of these two poems.
    What happened to the *nature* of war between the writing of the two poems?

▷   Do you think one of the poets is more 'serious' than the other?
    Give your reasons.
    How would you sum up their different attitudes to war?

▷   See if you can express in your own words how Brooke feels about duty.
    What religious beliefs do you suppose Brooke had?
    Does the way you regard Brooke's poem alter when you know that the young
    poet died while on active service, in 1915?

▷   Does your reading of the second poem take into account that the writer was
    unlikely to be called upon to fight for his country?
    How would you sum up the points McGough is making about patriotism in the
    first eight lines of his poem?
    How far do you agree with him?
    How would you describe McGough's attitude to life?
    Does that make you question anything in the first poem?

▷   How does McGough's attitude to death differ from Brooke's?

    Read the poems again now to see exactly what separates the two poets'
    outlooks before you choose an assignment.

Assignments

English

○ *Red, White and Blue Tinted Spectacles*
Write an essay or a poem in which you set out your own attitude to patriotism.
Do we all now live in a 'global village' where it is dangerous and irrelevant to
believe in 'My Country Right or Wrong'?
Or are there things British for which you would be prepared to fight and, if
necessary, to die?

English Literature

○ Essay: Does one of these two poems speak more strongly for you?
Examine the values expressed in each poem and explain where you stand in
relation to them.

○ Write an answer to either poem, in verse or prose, imitating the style of the
original.

Browning
THE PATRIOT

In the speech taken from *As You Like It* (p.6), fame or reputation was described as a 'bubble'. What do you think was meant by that?

Can you think of anyone who was famous one day and forgotten very shortly afterwards? Or of someone who for a while was very popular only to become very quickly the person everyone loved to hate?

Why do you think public opinion sometimes shifts so dramatically?

Do you think you would enjoy being famous?
What might be some of the pleasures and pains of being a public figure?

Read through the following poem carefully two or three times and then consider the points which follow.

The Patriot

An old story

It was roses, roses all the way,	
With myrtle mixed in my path like mad:	***myrtle*** *a fragrant shrub, an emblem of love.*
The house-roofs seemed to heave and sway,	
The church-spires flamed, such flags they had,	
A year ago on this very day. 5	
The air broke into a mist with bells,	
The old walls rocked with the crowd and cries,	
Had I said, 'Good folk, mere noise repels –	
But give me your sun from yonder skies!'	
They had answered, 'And afterward, what else?' 10	
Alack, it was I who leaped at the sun	***alack*** *alas.*
To give it my loving friends to keep!	
Nought man could do, have I left undone:	***nought*** *nothing.*
And you see my harvest, what I reap	
This very day, now a year is run. 15	
There's nobody on the house-tops now –	
Just a palsied few at the windows set;	***palsied*** *invalid.*
For the best of the sight is, all allow,	***allow*** *agree.*
At the Shambles' Gate – or, better yet,	***Shambles*** *slaughterhouse.*
By the very scaffold's foot, I trow. 20	***scaffold*** *place of execution.* ***trow*** *believe.*

I go in the rain, and, more than needs,
    A rope cuts both my wrists behind;
And I think, by the feel, my forehead bleeds
    For they fling, whoever has a mind,
Stones at me for my year's misdeeds.   *25*

Thus I entered, and thus I go!
    In triumphs, people have dropped down dead.
'Paid by the world, what dost thou owe
    Me?' – God might question; now instead
'Tis God shall repay: I am safer so.

more than needs
unnecessarily.

Thinking/Talking Points

▷   What is a patriot?
What do you imagine the speaker might have done to earn him the reception
he describes in the first two stanzas?
Which details capture the mood of the town, the scale of his popularity?

▷   What do you think the speaker means when he says:
'Had I said
        ". . . give me your sun from yonder skies!"
They had answered, "And afterward, what else?"'

▷   What significance does the phrase
'A year ago on this very day'
take on when you read the poem for a second time?

▷   We are not given a detailed account of what happened in the year following his
triumph but the third stanza gives us the Patriot's view of how he behaved. Can
you explain in your own words what he tried to do and why, perhaps, he made
himself unpopular?

▷   Look again at stanzas 4 and 5.
What procession does the Patriot find himself in now?
Which details emphasise his loneliness and misery, and the violent turnabout
in public opinion?

▷   How would you describe the Patriot's feelings in the final stanza?
What impression of his personality are you left with?

▷   Do you think this poem has 'a point to make'? If so, what?
Do you find it a convincing story?

Reread *The Patriot* before you choose your assignment.

Assignments

English

○ Individually or in a small group, produce two newspaper front pages, one for the day of the Patriot's homecoming, one for the day of his death.
Yours is a popular newspaper which reflects/helps to shape public opinion.
In the first report, give the readers plenty of 'facts' about the hero's background, daring exploits and 'remarkable achievements' and then, in the second front page, some account of the scandal or corruption which has led to his 'thoroughly deserved humiliation and execution'.

○ *A Child's Eye-Witness Account*
You were taken by your parents to cheer the National Hero home. You peeped into the streets on the day of the execution.
Write an account of what you saw and heard on each occasion as two diary entries.
Is it hard to understand why all the agreeable things they said about the man on the day of the victory parade have now been forgotten?

○ Rewrite this poem as a short story, filling out the details in the Patriot's biography.

○ Recast the poem (in verse or as a short story) as a story about the rise and fall of another kind of popular hero (e.g. a sportsman/woman; a rock star; an actor; a politician; a comic).

★

HOT NIGHT
ON WATER STREET
and
AFTER MIDNIGHT

Compare the way these two poems create the atmosphere of particular places at particular times.

Hot Night on Water Street

A hot midsummer night on Water Street –
The boys in jeans were combing their blond hair,
Watching the girls go by on tired feet;
And an old woman with a witch's stare
Cried 'Praise the Lord!' She vanished on a bus   *5*
With hissing air brakes, like an incubus.   **incubus** *demon.*

Three hardware stores, a barbershop, a bar,
A movie playing Westerns – where I went
To see a dream of horses called *The Star* . . .
Some day, when this uncertain continent   *10*
Is marble, and men ask what was the good
We lived by, dust may whisper 'Hollywood'.

Then back along the river bank on foot
By moonlight . . . On the West Virginia side
An owlish train began to huff and hoot;   *15*
It seemed to know of something that had died.
I didn't linger – sometimes when I travel
I think I'm being followed by the Devil.

At the newsstand in the lobby, a cigar
Was talkative: 'Since I've been in this town   *20*
I've seen one likely woman, and a car
As she was crossing Main Street knocked her down.'
I was a stranger here myself, I said,
And bought the New York Times, and went to bed.

☆

After Midnight

The dark streets are deserted,
With only a drugstore glowing
Softly, like a sleeping body;

With one white, naked bulb
In the back, that shines   5
On suicides and abortions.

Who lives in these dark houses?
I am suddenly aware
I might live here myself.

The garage man returns   10
And puts the change in my hand,
Counting the singles carefully.

Thinking/Talking Points

▷ Choose three or four descriptive details from *Hot Night on Water Street* and think
about *how* they conjure up a picture or a feeling.

▷ Do you find the woman who cries 'Praise the Lord!' sinister or comforting?
Can you explain why?

▷ Why do you think the poet chose to describe the man who smoked it as
'a cigar'?
What sort of man do you imagine?

▷ See if you can explain *how* the last stanza of *After Midnight* achieves its effect.

Assignments

English

○ *A Day in the Life*
Write a series of poems which capture the mood of a particular place at
different times of the day and night.
Avoid too much action or too much comment on what you 'photograph'.
Think of what your ears, nose and skin register as well as what your eyes see.

○ Choose one of these scenes as the setting for a short story. Be careful to
provide the reader with more crisp descriptive details as the story unfolds.

★

Yevtushenko
LIES

Sandburg
WHAT KIND OF LIAR ARE YOU?

'The truth is rarely pure, and never simple.'

Oscar Wilde

'There are three kinds of lies: lies, damned lies and statistics.'

Benjamin Disraeli

'When I was a little boy, they called me a liar;
but now I am grown up they call me a writer.'

Isaac Bashevis Singer

'We did not tell lies. But we did not tell the whole story.'

Sir Frank Cooper,
British defence chief, on the Falklands War

'[The letter] . . . contains a misleading impression, not a lie.
It was being economical with the truth.'

Sir Robert Armstrong,
Secretary to the British Cabinet and Head of the Civil Service,
during an exchange in the *Spycatcher* hearings

What kind of liar are you?
Told any good lies lately?
Is failing to tell the whole truth the same as lying?
Can you remember particular lies, half-truths, fibs you regret having told?

Are there lies you would justify?
What would you say to a toddler who asked,
  'There is a Father Christmas, isn't there?'
or to someone with terminal cancer, who asked,
  'Do you think I'm dying?'

What kind of liar are you?
What circumstances can lead us into lies?
Can you imagine a situation where telling the truth could be dangerous?

Are there lies you want to believe?
Do you tell yourself lies?
What do you suppose Eliot meant when he wrote,
  'Human kind cannot bear very much reality'?

What kind of liar are you?
Is there a moral difference between private lies and public lies?

Advertising has been called 'organised lying'.
Is government propaganda simply a pack of lies?
And what about packaging, legal wrangling, debating, canvassing, preaching,
the news, school reports, novels, pop songs and love letters?
Are we often told the truth, the whole truth and nothing but the truth?

What kind of liar are you?
What would you call someone who said, 'I never tell lies'?

Read through the following poem carefully two or three times before looking
at the points which follow.

Lies

Telling lies to the young is wrong.
Proving to them that lies are true is wrong.
Telling them that God's in his heaven
and all's well with the world is wrong.
The young know what you mean. The young are people.   *5*
Tell them the difficulties can't be counted,
and let them see not only what will be
but see with clarity these present times.
Say obstacles exist they must encounter
sorrow happens, hardship happens.   *10*
The hell with it. Who never knew
the price of happiness will not be happy.
Forgive no error you recognize,
it will repeat itself, increase,
and afterwards our pupils   *15*
will not forgive in us what we forgave.

Thinking/Talking Points

▷   Can you think of different *kinds* of lie told to the young by each of the
following?
parents   politicians   friends
teachers   the mass-media
Can you remember the first time you realised that adults could tell lies?

▷   Think of an example of when you were given a 'proof' that something was
other than it is. (Think about how people can 'lie with statistics' or tell you only
half a story to 'prove' a point.)

▷   What 'lie' about God is the poet referring to in lines 3–4?
How can 'God' be used to justify things which are unjust? (Think, for example,
what the phrase 'With God on our side' might mean to different people in
Northern Ireland, in the Punjab or in South Africa.)

▷ What does the poet feel is the proper way to talk to the young?
Do you agree with him?

▷ What do you think he means here:
               'Who never knew
the price of happiness will not be happy.'?
Do you think he's right? Think of a personal experience like that.

Assignments

English

○ *Organised Lying*
  (a) Find four or five examples of public lying (e.g. in newspapers, on television or on the radio).
      Describe the lies and examine *how* they are being told.
      Examine the purpose of each lie (e.g. to make a profit, to win power, to create a sensation, to avoid embarrassment).
  (b) Write an advertisement, a political speech or a pop-song which cunningly distorts the truth in order to exploit young children (imagine an audience of eight-year-olds).

○ Write a fairy-story which tries to frighten children into believing it is wicked to ask too many questions.

○ Write the conversation in which a twelve-year-old asks his mother or father about 'the facts of life' (or about 'the facts of death').

○ Essay: 'The basic aim of popular culture is to sell lies to the young for huge profits.'
  Discuss, with close reference to three or four examples.

○ *The Truth Pure and Simple*
  See if you can explain the truth about one of the following things in language which you think an eight-year-old would understand: reproduction; death; nuclear weapons; why children should not trust strangers.

○ Write a story to illustrate one of the varieties of lying described in the following poem by Carl Sandburg:

What Kind of Liar Are You?

                                              What kind of liar are you?
People lie because they don't remember clear what they saw.
People lie because they can't help making a story better than it was the
                                              way it happened.
People tell 'white lies' so as to be decent to others.
People lie in a pinch, hating to do it, but lying on because it might be worse.
And people lie just to be liars for a crooked personal gain.
    Which sort of a liar are you?
    Which of these liars are you?

★

A POLISHED PERFORMANCE

How many different meanings can you think of for the word 'polished'?
(e.g. Consider the way(s) it might be used about the following: furniture;
a sportsman's or an actor's performance; a lens; a trick; someone's appearance;
a political speech; a work of art; manners.)

Read through the following poem carefully two or three times before thinking
about the points which follow.

A Polished Performance

Citizens of the polished capital
  Sigh for the towns up country,
And their innocent simplicity.

People in the towns up country
  Applaud the unpolished innocence   5
Of the distant villages.

Dwellers in the distant villages
  Speak of a simple unspoilt girl,
Living alone, deep in the bush.

Deep in the bush we found her,   10
  Large and innocent of eye,
Among gentle gibbons and mountain ferns.

Perfect for the part, perfect,
  Except for the dropsy   *dropsy a disease in which*
Which comes from polished rice.   15 *fluid collects in the tissues.*

In the capital our film is much admired,
  Its gentle gibbons and mountain ferns,
Unspoilt, unpolished, large and innocent of eye.

☆

Thinking/Talking Points

▷   What do you notice about the ways the word 'polished' is used in the poem?
Can you suggest alternative ways of saying the following: a polished
performance; the polished capital; unpolished innocence; polished rice?

▷ We are told about a number of different types of people in the poem:
'Citizens . . . People . . . Dwellers . . . a simple . . . girl . . . Living alone . . .'
In what ways are they different?
What sorts of places do they live in?
How do the various groups feel about each other?

▷ 'Innocent simplicity . . . unpolished innocence . . . simple unspoilt . . .'
Jot down in your own words what you understand by these phrases.
How can these qualities be both good and bad?

▷ What *exactly* do the film makers find 'Deep in the bush'?
What does the phrase 'Perfect for the part' suggest to you about the kind of film they are making?
For whose benefit do you think it is being made?
What do you think the audience wants to see?

▷ What do you notice about the film which is finally shown?
How is it received?
In what sense(s) is it 'polished'?

▷ Can you suggest two possible interpretations of the poem's last three words?
(who/what could they be describing?)

▷ In what sense(s) is the poem itself 'A Polished Performance'?
Why do you think it was written?

Reread the poem now a couple of times to see what else needs thinking about before you choose an assignment. Think about the tone of voice in which the poem would be most effective, read aloud.

Assignments

English

○ *Meet the Director*
Drawing on the poem but adding lots of your own ideas, imagine you are the director, commissioned to produce the kind of film which will be a box-office success in 'the polished capital'.
In an interview on a popular chat show, describe some of the problems you had to solve, shooting and editing the film. (He/she will probably be a 'polished' performer.)

○ *Promises*
Write a story about the impact made upon a simple, 'backward' society by the arrival of 'civilisation'.
See if you can bring out how both 'progress' and 'innocent simplicity' can be good and bad things.

English Literature

○ Essay: In what senses is this poem 'A Polished Performance'?
What do you think Enright's purpose was in writing it?
Do you think he has been successful?
Remember to refer closely to the text in your answer.

Gunn

THE PRODUCE DISTRICT

Read through the following poem carefully three or four times before thinking about the assignment.

The Produce District

What's there to do on Sundays? Sooner do this than booze.

After the businesses had moved, before
The wrecking started
For the high-rise blocks:
An interim:
Whoever walked along these streets   5
Found it was shared with him
Only by pigeons, single or in flocks.

Where each night trucks had waited
By warehouse and worn ramp
With oranges or celery to unload,   10
Now it was smell of must, rot, fungus, damp.
The crumbling and decay accelerated,
Old mattresses and boards in heaps
Losing their colours with their shapes.
The smaller things   15
Blending like humus, on the road.
And silence – no, small creaks,
Small patterings,
While now, above, the thump and whirr of wings.
The pigeons, grey on grey,   20
In greater number
Than ever here before
Pecked round the rotting lumber
Perched on the roofs and walls,
Or wheeled between the faded signs   25
And broken ornamental scrolls.

I watched the work of spiders, rats and rain,
And turning on to Front Street found
I was not there alone.
He stood unmoving on the littered ground   30
In bright scrubbed denims
An airgun loosely in his hands
Staring at something overhead.

interim a pause, a temporary state of affairs.

must mould, mustiness.

blending like humus decomposing, mixing together like compost.

lumber discarded furniture, rubbish.

scrolls decorative stone or timber resembling rolled-up parchment.

Shooting at birds, he said.
I looked at his short greying hair;   35
His face, lined, hard and ruddy, any age,
Cracking into a smile;
And stood beside him while
He aimed at a parapet some forty-five yards off.   **parapet** *low wall running*
A bang. One pigeon as the others rose   40   *along a balcony.*
A lump of fluff
Dropped from among them lightly to the street.

Cool air, high fog, and underfoot
Through soft mould, shapes felt like uneven root
Ridging a forest floor.   45
The place losing itself, lost now, unnamed,
Birds wheeling back, with a low threshing sound.
He aimed
And then once more
I heard the gun repeat   50
Its accurate answer to the wilderness,
Echoing it and making it complete.
And maple shoots pushed upward through the ground.

Assignments

English

○ In verse or prose, write a continuation of the story of what happened to the
   district once 'the wrecking started' and then rebuilding began.

○ *All Change . . .*
   Imagine you are producing a radio documentary about the decline and
   reconstruction of an inner city area.
   (a) Invent some interviews with people who used to live and work there and
       with someone who still does.
   (b) Describe with a reporter's eye what you see, hear, and feel as you walk
       through the district.
       Comment on the dereliction and waste and on the curious atmosphere of a
       place which was once a hive of business, is due for redevelopment but is
       now an odd mixture of urban decay and returning wilderness.
   (c) Interview a cross-section of people with strong views about how the
       district should be rebuilt (e.g. a social worker; a property developer;
       a priest; some old people; some people of your age; a conservationist).
   (d) Leave the listeners with some speculations about what the district may be
       like in ten years' time.
   You could present your work on tape, as if it were a radio programme, or as a
   wall display, using pictures you've drawn or found in newspapers and
   magazines.

★

═══ *Eliot* ═══
PRELUDES

Do you think it matters where you live? Do you think it matters what the environment looks like?

Is Art just decoration? Nice to have but not really necessary?

How far do you agree with these ideas, expressed in 1859:

'The changes in this country are now so rapid that it would be absurd to lay down laws of art education under present circumstances; therefore I must ask, how much of it do you seriously intend within the next fifty years to be coal-pit, brick-field, or quarry? Let's suppose you have complete success: that from shore to shore the whole country is to be set as thick with chimneys as the masts that stand in the docks of Liverpool; that there shall be no meadows in it; no trees; no gardens; only a little corn grown upon the housetops, reaped and threshed by steam; that you do not even leave room for roads, but travel either over the roofs of your factories on bridges; or under their floors, in tunnels; that, smoke having rendered the light of the sun useless, you work always by the light of your own gas; that no acre of English ground shall be without its machinery and therefore no spot of English ground left on which it is possible to stand without risk of being blown into small pieces.

Under these circumstances, no beautiful art will be possible. Beautiful art can only be produced by people who have beautiful things about them and leisure to look at them; and unless you provide some elements of beauty for your workers to be surrounded by, you will find no elements of beauty can be invented by them.'

(Adapted from Ruskin *Modern Manufacture and Design*)

Assignment 1

○   If Ruskin were writing today, what do you think he would substitute for: coal-pit, brick-field, or quarry; chimneys; the masts in the docks of Liverpool; steam; gas?

○   See if you can produce an up-to-date piece like Ruskin's, written to suit present circumstances.

Assignment 2

○   This is an activity you may like to tackle in pairs.
On the opposite page are some lines from a poem about a day in the life of a city. Some words have been missed out. Suggest a word to go into each gap.

Preludes

I

The winter evening settles down
With ...... of ...... in passageways.
Six o'clock.
The ...... ends of ...... days.
And now a gusty shower wraps   *5*
The ...... scraps
Of ...... leaves about your feet
And ...... from ...... lots;
The showers beat
On ...... blinds and chimney-pots,   *10*
And at the corner of the street
A ...... cab-horse steams and stamps.

And then the lighting of the lamps.

II

The morning comes to ......
Of faint stale ...... of ......
From the ...... trampled street
With all its ...... feet that ......
To early ...... stands.   *5*

With the other ......
That time resumes,
One thinks of all the hands
That are raising ...... shades
In a thousand ...... rooms.   *10*

IV

His ...... stretched tight across the skies
That fade behind a city ......
Or trampled by ...... feet
At four and ...... and six o'clock.
And short ...... fingers ...... pipes,   *5*
And evening newspapers, and eyes
...... of ...... certainties,
The conscience of a ...... street
...... to ...... the world.

☆

Assignment 3

○ In Appendix 1 (page 164) you will find the actual words and phrases which have been omitted. See if you can decide where they went.

○ Which of Eliot's words were *most* like the ones you supplied?
Which words were *least* like your suggestions?
Which of Eliot's, and which of your own words do you think best capture the character of a city and its inhabitants?
Are there any of Eliot's words which seem to you to be out of character?

104

Thinking/Talking Points

▷ What mood does the phrase 'settle down' suggest to you?

▷ What is the effect of the abrupt third line?
(What seems to happen to the city at six o'clock?)

▷ Jot down six words of your own to describe the character of the place.

▷ At what tempo, in what tone of voice would you read the first line?

▷ Why 'sawdust-trampled'? (What was a spit-and-sawdust restaurant?)
Why do you think Eliot describes everything going on as a 'masquerade'?

▷ What are 'furnished rooms'? What does that imply about the city dwellers?

▷ In *Prelude I*, the inhabitants were identified only by their smells of cooking and litter; here merely as 'hands' and 'feet'.
What is the effect of describing them in that way?

▷ Whose soul can you see 'stretched tight across the skies'?
What is the effect of that vision on the city dwellers?

▷ Suggest what Eliot means when he says they are 'assured of *certain* certainties'?
Are we like them? What are some of your own 'certainties'?

▷ Suggest five or six words of your own to describe the lifestyle and the attitudes of these people. What do you think their idea of Heaven might be?

Further Assignments

English

○ *Prelude III* (fifteen lines long) has not been printed here. In it, the 'camera' which has been surveying the city zooms in through a window of one of the thousand furnished rooms and describes the waking-up of its tenant.
Write your own version of the missing poem.

○ Write a sequence of *Preludes* describing a place you know well.

English Literature

○ Eliot's *Preludes* are concise and impressionistic. What impression of the city and its population does each of them give you? Which words and phrases, which particular images are most graphic, most suggestive?

○ Turn to Appendix 2 on page 164.
Either (a) write a study of *Prelude III*
or (b) make a careful comparison of your version of *Prelude III* and Eliot's.

○ We have not printed here the final seven lines of *Prelude IV*. In those lines, the poet steps from behind the camera through which he has described everything so impersonally to tell us how he is affected by what he has 'seen'.
See if you can compose a fitting end to Eliot's sequence of poems.

○ Compare your own conclusion to the sequence with Eliot's, which you will find in Appendix 3 on page 164.

★

Auden
THE UNKNOWN CITIZEN

Following a war, countries sometimes erect a monument to an unknown soldier.
Why do you think they do this?

Before you read the following poem, see if you can imagine the circumstances in which such a monument might be put up.

Read the poem two or three times before considering the points below. Once you have grasped its general shape, think carefully about the tone of voice in which the poem should be read.

Thinking/Talking Points

▷   If you could see into the future and discovered that, after your death, the state put up a monument to you, how would you feel about it?
Would you feel differently if, instead of your name on the monument, there was a number?
What does the fact that this citizen is 'unknown', except as a number, suggest to you about the kind of country he lived in?

▷   What do the first two lines of the poem suggest to you about the kind of 'interest' this State takes in its citizens?

▷   How do you imagine a saint? How might a saint behave?
Who, alive today, would you call a saint?
Jot down some words to describe a saintly person.
What do you think the State in the poem means when it uses the word 'saint'?
List some of the qualities this State would regard as saintly.
How do you think it would treat a real saint?

▷   In what ways do you think the 'Union' we are told about in the poem differs in its duties and powers from trade unions in our country?

▷   Social psychologists study human behaviour.
How do you imagine they collected their data about JS/07/M378?

▷   What would be regarded as *normal* reactions to advertisements in JS/07/M378's society?
What word could you substitute for the word 'normal' in line 15?
Can you find any other words whose meaning the State has changed?

(*continued*)

The Unknown Citizen

To
JS/07/M378
This Marble Monument
Is erected by the State

He was found by the Bureau of Statistics to be
One against whom there was no official complaint,
And all the reports on his conduct agree
That, in the modern sense of an old-fashioned word, he was a saint,
For in everything he did he served the Greater Community.   *5*
Except for the War till the day he retired
He worked in a factory and never got fired,
But satisfied his employers, Fudge Motors Inc.
Yet he wasn't a scab or odd in his views,
For his Union reports that he paid his dues,   *10*
(Our report on his Union shows it was sound)
And our Social Psychology workers found
That he was popular with his mates and liked a drink.
The Press are convinced that he bought a paper every day
And that his reactions to advertisements were normal in every way.   *15*
Policies taken out in his name prove that he was fully insured,
And his Health-card shows he was once in hospital but left it cured.
Both Producers Research and High-Grade Living declare
He was fully sensible to the advantages of the Instalment Plan
And had everything necessary to the Modern Man,   *20*
A phonograph, a radio, a car and a frigidaire.
Our researchers into Public Opinion are content
That he held the proper opinions for the time of year;
When there was peace, he was for peace; when there was war, he went.
He was married and added five children to the population,   *25*
Which our Eugenist says was the right number for a parent of his generation
And our teachers report that he never interfered with their education.
Was he free? Was he happy? The question is absurd:
Had anything been wrong, we certainly should have heard.

bureau *office, department.*

statistics *facts and figures.*

he served the greater community *he worked for the good of others.*

a scab *a worker whose loyalty is more to the firm than to his mates in the union.*

dues *subscription.*

sound *healthy, reliable.*

social psychology workers *people who study human behaviour in groups.*

Producers Research *presumably a company which carries out market research.*

the instalment plan *hire purchase; buying goods on credit.*

phonograph *record player.*

frigidaire *fridge.*

Eugenist *someone who studies ways of 'improving' the nation by encouraging only those with desirable qualities to breed.*

▷ Think carefully about the difference between (a) *the quality of life* and (b) *the standard of living*.
Which of the two *can't* be measured by statistics?
Which do you think has more bearing on people's happiness?
Which do you think 'High-Grade Living' is interested in?

▷ Do you agree that the unknown citizen had 'everything necessary to the Modern Man'?
What important things are missing from the list?
Do you think 'High-Grade Living' could provide them?

▷ What do you think might happen if the Unknown Citizen had 'interfered' with his children's education?
What kind of education do you think they received?

▷ Suggest how JS/07/M378 might have died.

Reread the poem now, three or four times, to see if there are other points which deserve attention. Think again about how you think the poet intended the piece to be read.

Assignments

English

○ Write a short story called 'A Day in the Life and Death of JS/07/M378'.
Use details from the poem but add plenty of your own ideas to emphasise how much and how little freedom JS/07/M378 has.

English Literature

○ By referring closely to the text, describe the kind of State the Unknown Citizen lived in.
Would you be happy living in such a place?
Do you think it is in any ways like our own?

○ Essay: 'Was he free? Was he happy?'.
What would be your verdict on JS/07/M378?
Remember to refer closely to the text.

For further study

Compare and contrast the ideas explored in the poem with the concerns of Chapters XVI–XVII of Aldous Huxley's novel *Brave New World*.

Other texts on similar themes
E.M. Forster   *The Machine Stops*
Ray Bradbury   *Fahrenheit 451*
Michael Frayn   *The Tin Men*

★

AU JARDIN
DES PLANTES

Read through the following poem carefully three or four times before
considering the points which follow.

Au Jardin des Plantes

The gorilla lay on his back,
One hand cupped under his head,
Like a man.

Au Jardin des Plantes
at the zoo.

Like a labouring man tired with work,
A strong man with his strength burnt away   5
In the toil of earning a living.

toil hard work.

Only of course he was not tired out with work,
Merely with boredom; his terrible strength
All burnt away by prodigal idleness.

prodigal wasteful, lazy,
self-indulgent.

A thousand days, and then a thousand days   10
Idleness licked away his beautiful strength
He having no need to earn a living.

It was all laid on, free of charge.
We maintained him, not for doing anything,
But for being what he was.   15

And so that Sunday morning he lay on his back,
Like a man, like a worn-out man,
One hand cupped under his terrible hard head.

Like a man, like a man,
One of those we maintain, not for doing anything,   20
But for being what they are.

A thousand days, and then a thousand days,
With everything laid on, free of charge,
They cup their heads in prodigal idleness.

☆

Thinking/Talking Points

▷   How many differences can you think of between a human and a gorilla?
    What point do you think the poet is making by repeating the phrase 'Like a
    man, like a man' throughout the poem? In what tone of voice would you read
    the phrase?

▷   What attitude to work is expressed in the second stanza?
    Do you think there is another way of seeing work?

▷   See if you can put this into your own words:
                'his terrible strength
    All burnt away by prodigal idleness.'
    What do you think the poet is saying about the effects of doing nothing all day,
    day in, day out?

▷   What tone of voice do you hear in lines 13–15?
    How do you think the gorilla might respond to those lines were he able to
    understand them?

▷   Whom do you think the speaker has in mind in lines 20–21?
    How many years and months is 'a thousand days'?
    What is the effect of repeating the phrase?

    Read *Au Jardin des Plantes* again now a couple of times to see what other points
    need thinking about before you choose an assignment.

Assignments

English

○   *A Thousand Days and then a Thousand Days* . . .
    Write a poem or a piece of prose in which *either* this gorilla *or* someone
    unemployed reflects upon his/her way of life and compares it with that of the
    people who 'keep' him/her.

○   Essay: 'Prodigal Idleness'.
    Do you think unemployment is like an extended holiday?
    How do you think years of unemployment would affect you?
    What do you think you would feel about those in work?
    Write an essay examining the likely consequences of our becoming a society
    where some do and some don't have work.

English Literature

○   Essay: What attitudes to animals and to people do you think the poet is
    criticising in this poem? Do you sympathise with his point of view?
    How effective do you find the way John Wain has made his points?
    Remember to refer closely to the text in your answer.

★

DISABLED

Disabled people often complain that others 'see the wheelchair, not the person'.
Do you think that is sometimes true of you?
What prejudices, assumptions, attitudes do you find yourself slipping into when you encounter someone who is physically handicapped?
What do you think it would feel like to be stereotyped or simply ignored as no longer fully human?

Read through the following poem carefully two or three times before looking at the points which follow.

Disabled

He sat in a wheeled chair, waiting for dark,
And shivered in his ghastly suit of grey,
Legless, sewn short at elbow. Through the park
Voices of boys rang saddening like a hymn,
Voices of play and pleasure after day,   *5*
Till gathering sleep had mothered them from him.

About this time Town used to swing so gay
When glow-lamps budded in the light blue trees,   **glow-lamps** *incandescent lamps.*
And girls glanced lovelier as the air grew dim, –
In the old times, before he threw away his knees.   *10*
Now he will never feel again how slim
Girls' waists are, or how warm their subtle hands;   **subtle** *sensitive, gentle.*
All of them touch him like some queer disease.

There was an artist silly for his face,   **silly for his face** *eager to draw him.*
For it was younger than his youth, last year.   *15*
Now, he is old; his back will never brace;   **brace** *be upright.*
He's lost his colour very far from here,
Poured it down shell-holes till the veins ran dry,
And half his lifetime lapsed in the hot race,   **lapsed** *passed away.*
And leap of purple spurted from his thigh.   *20*

One time he liked a blood-smear down his leg,
After the matches, carried shoulder-high.
It was after football, when he'd drunk a peg,   **peg** *a drink, probably brandy and soda.*
He thought he'd better join. – He wonders why,
Someone had said he'd look a god in kilts,   *25*
That's why; and may be, too, to please his Meg;
Aye, that was it, to please the giddy jilts   **giddy jilts** *silly, flirtatious girls.*
He asked to join. He didn't have to beg;

111

Smiling they wrote his lie; aged nineteen years.
Germans he scarcely thought of; all their guilt,   30
And Austria's, did not move him. And no fears
Of Fear came yet. He thought of jewelled hilts   **hilts** *handles of daggers.*
For daggers in plaid socks; of smart salutes;   **plaid** *tartan.*
And care of arms; and leave; and pay arrears;
Esprit de corps; and hints for young recruits.   35   **esprit de corps** *team-spirit,*
And soon, he was drafted out with drums and cheers.   *companionship.*
Some cheered him home, but not as crowds cheer Goal.
Only a solemn man who brought him fruits
Thanked him; and then inquired about his soul.

Now, he will spend a few sick years in Institutes,   40
And do what things the rules consider wise,
And take whatever pity they may dole.   **dole** *hand out.*
To-night he noticed how the women's eyes
Passed from him to the strong men that were whole.
How cold and late it is! Why don't they come   45
And put him into bed? Why don't they come?

Thinking/Talking Points

▷ 'They see the chair, not the person.'
Did you find the phrase 'a wheeled chair' suggested a certain sort of person
to you?
How does the way this man is dressed help to make him a *type* rather than a
person?

▷ Look again at lines 1–2 and lines 40–42.
What points do you think the poet is making about 'Institutes'?

▷ 'waiting for dark'
What does this phrase suggest to you?

▷ 'Legless, sewn short at elbow.'
Why do you think the poet chose to present these facts to us so abruptly?

▷ Look again at lines 4–6.
What do they add to your impression of the disabled man's situation?
Why do we *have to* refer to the subject of this poem as 'the disabled man'?

▷ Look again at lines 7–9.
What impression of 'the old times' do these lines give you?
Can you describe *how* they do it?

▷ How did you react when you read the phrase 'he threw away his knees'?
Did any other phrases in the poem have a similar effect upon you?

▷ Are you able to sympathise with the girls' attitude to the disabled man?

▷ Look again at stanza 4.
Who do you think was most to blame for the man's mutilation?

▷ Look again at lines 38–39.
   What impression does the poet give us of the man who 'thanked' the soldier?

▷ What do you feel for the disabled man as you read the last two lines of the poem?

Read the poem again now to see what other points are worth attention before you choose an assignment.

Assignments

English

○ *Chin Up!*
Write a story or poem about a young man or woman permanently crippled (e.g. in a game, whilst climbing a tree for a dare, in a motorcycle crash or in an accident at work.)
Bring out the way the attitudes of others – friends, girl/boyfriend, family – gradually change as they realise he/she will never fully recover.
Bring out, too, the disabled person's own changing feelings about those around him/her and about the label, 'disabled'.

English Literature

○ Essay: 'The Chair, Not the Person'.
How does Owen make us share something of the loss, the indignity and the pain of the disabled in this poem?
Has the poem helped you to understand the feelings of people confined to wheelchairs?
Remember to refer to the text in your answer.

Further reading

Kafka   Short story   *Metamorphosis*

★

FAIRY TALE

'. . . lives in a world of her/his own'

Might someone say that about you?
What is the 'world of your own' like?
What unpleasant bits of life do you shut out?
What special furniture does it contain?

Have you ever slipped into the trap of confusing a daydream with reality?
What do you think happens to people who live in a permanent fantasy?

Fairy Tale

He built himself a house,
    his foundations,
    his stones,
    his walls,
    his roof overhead,   5
    his chimney and smoke,
    his view from the window.

He made himself a garden,
    his fence,
    his thyme,   10   **thyme** *a fragrant herb.*
    his earthworm,
    his evening dew.

He cut out his bit of sky above.

And he wrapped the garden in the sky
and the house in the garden   15
and packed the lot in a handkerchief

and went off
lone as an arctic fox   **lone** *lonely.*
through the cold
unending   20
rain
into the world.

☆

Thinking/Talking Points

▷ What kind of house do you daydream about?
What kind of world?
What kind of people?

▷ Do your fantasies keep changing?
What do your fantasies reveal about your personality?

▷ If you/they are willing to share them, you may like to compare your daydreams with those of your friends.
Is it easy to predict each other's fantasies?

▷ What sorts of dream-worlds can you imagine each of the following creating for themselves: a long-distance lorry driver; a housewife; a shop assistant; somebody about to join the army; an old person living in a high-rise flat; someone about to play for the school team for the first time; an office-worker; someone who's blind; a tax inspector; a schoolteacher; a prime minister; an abandoned child; a police officer.

▷ How would you describe the poet's attitude to the man in *Fairy Tale*?
Do you think writing poetry is like daydreaming?

▷ 'lone . . .
into the world'
sounds like a contradiction. Is it?
How would you describe the man's situation at the end of the poem?

Read the poem again now before you choose an assignment.

Assignments

English

○ *A Day in the Life and Dreams of Mr/Mrs/Miss/Ms Grey*
Mr/Mrs/Miss/Ms Grey lives in the Flats, works at Dead Ends, eats at Blands . . .
But inside is a butterfly/tiger/snake/poet struggling to get out.
See if you can write a story which switches its attention between what a very ordinary-seeming person does and what he/she is thinking, dreaming about.

○ If there were half-a-dozen things you could achieve simply by willing them into being, what would they be?
Write your own *Fairy Tale* in verse or prose.

Some other works which explore this theme:

Short stories:
    Peter Bichsel   *A Table is a Table*
    James Thurber   *The Secret Life of Walter Mitty*
Film
    Woody Allen   *The Purple Rose of Cairo*

★

Gunn
ON THE MOVE

What does the word 'uniform' mean to you?
What are some of the reasons why people wear uniforms?
How many different kinds of uniform can you think of?
What do you think happens to a person when he/she puts one on?
Which uniforms do you wear?

How many different meanings can you think of for the word 'movement'?

In this poem, Thom Gunn explores what it is like to be born into the second half of the twentieth century. Many things which were 'certain' for people in the past are now more open to question.

Think about what has happened to the various groups that people used to belong to: the Church; the family; the neighbourhood; the social class; the nation. All these groups are much more splintered and unstable now than they used to be.

Darwin, Marx, Freud and Einstein, whatever they contributed to the sum of human knowledge, above all contributed doubt, scepticism. We are much less prepared than people were a hundred years ago to accept things as true simply because they appear to be true.

It is increasingly difficult for young people to decide whom to respect or follow, whose judgement to trust. Think about how much more information (and misinformation) you have to deal with each day than had to be coped with even when your parents were young. Being human involves making enormous numbers of choices and often it is not clear when the choice you make is right or wrong.

Animals, by contrast, appear to have no problems; they have their life-programme given to them: instinct. A cow doesn't spend too much time worrying about a career, politics or the meaning of life. If it's hungry it eats, if it's tired it sleeps.

Gunn sees the Human Condition as lonely, demanding, challenging but above all exciting. The risks and doubts are the price we pay for being free to shape our own destinies. Will is infinitely superior to instinct.

Read through the poem carefully three or four times before considering the points which follow.

On the Move

'Man you gotta go'

The blue jay scuffling in the bushes follows
Some hidden purpose, and the gust of birds
That spurts across the field, the wheeling swallows,
Have nested in the trees and undergrowth.
Seeking their instinct, or their poise, or both,   5
One moves with an uncertain violence
Under the dust thrown by a baffled sense
Or the dull thunder of approximate words.

On motorcycles, up the road, they come:
Small, black, as flies hanging in heat, the Boys,   10
Until the distance throws them forth, their hum
Bulges to thunder held by calf and thigh.
In goggles, donned impersonality,
In gleaming jackets trophied with the dust,
They strap in doubt – by hiding it, robust –   15
And almost hear a meaning in their noise.

Exact conclusion of their hardiness
Has no shape yet, but from known whereabouts
They ride, direction where the tires press.
They scare a flight of birds across the field: 20
Much that is natural, to the will must yield.
Men manufacture both machine and soul,
And use what they imperfectly control
To dare a future from the taken routes.

It is a part solution, after all.   25
One is not necessarily discord
On earth; or damned because, half animal,
One lacks direct instinct, because one wakes
Afloat on movement that divides and breaks.
One joins the movement in a valueless world,   30
Choosing it, till both hurler and the hurled,
One moves as well, always toward, toward.

A minute holds them, who have come to go:
The self-defined, astride the created will
They burst away; the towns they travel through   35
Are home for neither bird nor holiness,
For birds and saints complete their purposes.
At worst, one is in motion; and at best,
Reaching no absolute, in which to rest,
One is always nearer by not keeping still.

☆

spurts suddenly accelerates.
wheeling circling.

donned put on.
impersonality anonymity.

robust strong.

conclusion purpose, end.
hardiness boldness, toughness.
tires the American spelling of 'tyres'.

discord out of place.

astride riding on.

absolute perfection, stability, final answer.

Thinking/Talking Points

▷ What mood, what outlook upon life is suggested by the snatch of a pop song we're given in the epigraph 'Man, you gotta go'?

▷ Look again at stanza 1.
What is so different about the ways swallows and men move?
Why are words only 'approximate'?
Which words and images connect the speaker with 'the Boys'?
Think about this connection as you explore the poem.

▷ Look at the second stanza again.
How does the poet capture the sense of the boys' movement?
How do you react to the way they are first described:
'Small, black, as flies . . .'?
What does the phrase 'the distance throws them forth' suggest to you about the boys' control over their lives?
What mixture of feelings does this phrase suggest to you:
'thunder held by calf and thigh'?
What do you understand by the phrases 'donned impersonality' and 'strap in doubt'?
How can dust be like a trophy?
What do you think the poet is saying about the boys' state of mind when he says they '*almost* hear a meaning in their noise'?
Which line from stanza 1 does this recall?

▷ Look again at stanza 3.
What do you think the phrase 'direction where the tires press' means?
'Much that is natural, to the will must yield'
What do you think the poet is saying here about the basic differences between men and animals?
Do you think people can 'manufacture' their souls?

▷ Reread the last two stanzas.
Why do you think what the boys are doing is only 'a part solution'?
What do you think the problem was?
                              'one wakes
Afloat on movement that divides and breaks.'
What image(s) do you see here?
Into what kinds of 'movement' do you think you were born?
Which of the following do you think comes closest to what Gunn means here by a 'valueless world': (a) a worthless world, (b) a world with no fixed values, or (c) a priceless world?

▷ Why does the poet think movement is better than 'keeping still'?
Do you agree with him?

Reread the poem a couple of times now to see what other points deserve thinking about before you choose an assignment.
What attitude to the boys do you think the poet has? How is he like them?

Assignments

English

○ Draw or paint a picture suggested by the poem.

○ *On the Road*
Write a monologue, the private observations, thoughts, reflections of one of the boys as he rides from one town to another.

○ *A Lost Generation*
Write an imaginary interview with one of the boys, in which a middle-aged reporter tries to discover 'what makes the boys tick'.

English Literature

○ Describe and discuss the various sorts of 'movement' examined in Gunn's poem.

○ What does this poem say about the differences between men and animals? Do you agree with the idea, 'Much that is natural, to the will must yield'? Remember to refer closely to the text in your answer.

○ Show how Gunn sees 'the Boys' as representative of young people today. What problems do they face? What *solution* do the boys find? How satisfactory do you think that solution is? Remember to refer closely to the text in your answer.

Some other works which explore this theme:

Gunn   *The Unsettled Motorcyclist's Vision of his Death*
            The Human Condition

Films:
Ray   *Rebel Without a Cause*
Benedet   *The Wild One*

★

Shakespeare
from MACBETH

Would you describe yourself as ambitious? Do you think ambition is healthy? Can it be evil?

What sort of person do you imagine when someone says, 'Oh, X is really ambitious'?

Have you been given any advice about your ambitions – at home, in school, from friends, by the media?

Do you think ambitious people are more likely or less likely to be happy people? Do you enjoy their company?

What follows is an extract from a play in which a successful and popular man, Macbeth, is torn by conflicting feelings. He wants more than anything to be King. He has, staying under his roof, Duncan, the King who has shown him nothing but kindness. The opportunity to murder his guest and steal the crown has been one for which Macbeth has long waited. Such a chance may never present itself again. Macbeth leaves the banquet he's giving for the trusting King, to try to clarify his own thoughts.

Read through the soliloquy carefully a few times and give yourself time to think about it before considering the points which follow.

Soliloquy

If it were done when 'tis done, then 'twere well
It were done quickly. If th'assassination
Could trammel up the consequence, and catch,
With his surcease, success; that but this blow
Might be the be-all and the end-all – here,   5
But here, upon this bank and shoal of time,
We'd jump the life to come. – But in these cases,
We still have judgement here; that we but teach
Bloody instructions, which, being taught, return
To plague th'inventor: this even-handed Justice   10
Commends th'ingredients of our poison'd chalice
To our own lips. He's here in double trust:
First, as I am his kinsman and his subject,
Strong both against the deed; then, as his host,
Who should against his murderer shut the door,   15
Not bear the knife myself. Besides, this Duncan
Hath borne his faculties so meek, hath been
So clear in his great office, that his virtues
Will plead like angels, trumpet-tongu'd, against
The deep damnation of his taking-off;   20
And Pity, like a naked newborn babe,

soliloquy a speech in which a character in a play speaks his thoughts aloud.
trammel up control or catch up in the same net.
surcease death.

shoal sandbank or a place where the water is shallow.

commends offers.
chalice cup or goblet.

borne his faculties exercised his power.
meek gently, humbly.
clear irreproachable.
taking-off murder.

Striding the blast, or heaven's Cherubin hors'd
Upon the sightless couriers of the air,
Shall blow the horrid deed in every eye,
That tears shall drown the wind. – I have no spur   25
To prick the sides of my intent, but only
Vaulting ambition, which o'er leaps itself
And falls on th'other –

cherubin angels, probably
looking like beautiful
children.
sightless couriers the
winds.

from *Macbeth* Act I sc. vii

☆

Thinking/Talking Points

▷ What does the rhythm and punctuation of the opening two lines suggest to you
about the speaker's (Macbeth's) state of mind?

▷ Look at lines 2–12.
   (a) What do you understand by the phrase 'the life to come'?
       What do you think Macbeth means when he says he'd 'jump' it?
   (b) If we live on 'this bank and shoal of time', what image is the speaker
       suggesting represents 'the life to come' (Eternity)?
       What would happen if someone tried to jump that?
   Nevertheless, Macbeth says: If I could be sure that when I struck the blow
   that killed him, that would be the end of the matter as far as this world was
   concerned, I'd be willing to risk what might happen to me afterwards.
   (c) What new line of reasoning comes in with the word 'But' (line 7)?
       What does Macbeth believe happens to people who murder? (see lines 7–12).

▷ Look again at lines 12–25.
   (a) Macbeth is trying to give himself 'reasons' why he shouldn't murder the
       old man. Can you put them into your own words?
   (b) Against these 'reasons', Macbeth paints a picture of ambition.
       What do you see happening here:
       'Vaulting ambition, which o'erleaps itself
       And falls on th'other . . .' [side]
       (Think of a man showing off as he mounts his horse or urges his horse over
       a high fence.)
       What is Macbeth saying ambition does to a man?
   (c) What conclusion has he apparently reached?
       How would you describe Macbeth's state of mind at the end of this soliloquy?

Read the whole soliloquy again before thinking about these further points:

▷ Macbeth said he'd 'jump the life to come' if he could enjoy security in his
lifetime. 'Jump' suggests taking a risk . . . perhaps there is no 'life to come'?;
perhaps it would turn out all right anyway?
Did you notice that when he was giving himself 'reasons' for not killing
Duncan, Macbeth's language was full of pictures?
Can you imagine a scene in which there are: angels, trumpet-tongu'd . . . Pity,
like a newborn babe, striding . . . heaven's Cherubin . . . tears (that) . . . drown
the wind?

▷   Look at the picture on page 123. What do you think is happening?
    What is Shakespeare revealing about Macbeth's deepest thoughts about 'the
    life to come'?
    How is the image 'jump the life to come' connected to the one with which the
    soliloquy ends?
    What 'reason' do you think has really made him think again about the murder?

    Reread the soliloquy a few times before you choose an assignment.
    In what sort of voice, at what pace and volume would you deliver these lines?

Assignments

English

○   See if you can 'rewrite' this scene in verse or prose as if it came from a
    modern play in which a high-flying executive battles with his mixed feelings
    about his boss, staying the night in his house.

○   In the next part of this scene from *Macbeth*, Lady Macbeth, who has shared the
    ambitious plot of her husband, comes in. Macbeth tells her he has decided not
    to go through with their plan to murder Duncan. She is furious, argues with
    him, counters every argument he puts forward, changes his mind again.
    In verse or prose, see if you can write that scene, in 'Shakespearean' or in
    modern English.

English Literature

○   Describe the conflicting thoughts and feelings running through the speaker's
    mind in this soliloquy.
    Refer closely to the text.

○   Compare Shakespeare's text with the following version in modern English by
    Alan Durban.
    Begin by examining whether the prose sense of the two passages is the same.
    Then consider whether anything has been 'lost' in the translation from poetry
    into prose.

    If when it's done, that's the end of it, then the quicker it's done, the better. If the killing
    of the King had no consequences, and his death ensured success . . . if, when I struck
    the blow, that would be the job finished and the end of it . . . here, right here, on this
    side of eternity . . . we'd chance the life to come. But usually, we get what's coming
    here on earth. We teach the art of bloodshed, then become the victims of our own
    lessons. Impartial Justice makes us swallow our own poison, *(Pause)* Duncan is here on
    double trust. First, because I'm his kinsman and his subject – two good arguments
    against the deed. Then because I'm his host. I ought to protect him from his murderer,
    not carry the knife myself. Besides, this Duncan has used his power so gently, he's been
    so incorruptible in his great office, that his virtues will plead like angels, their tongues
    trumpeting the damnable horror of his murder. It would be as pitiful as if a new-born
    baby were exposed to a storm, or angels were subject to a hurricane. Tears would blind
    the eye and drown the wind! I've nothing to spur me on but high-leaping ambition,
    which can often bring about one's downfall.

    from *Shakespeare Made Easy: Macbeth* (Hutchinson)

★

HAWK ROOSTING

Read through the following poem carefully three or four times before considering the points which follow.

Hawk Roosting

I sit in the top of the wood, my eyes closed.
Inaction, no falsifying dream
Between my hooked head and hooked feet:
Or in sleep rehearse perfect kills and eat.

no falsifying dream no deflusions or illusions.

The convenience of the high trees!   5
The air's buoyancy and the sun's ray
Are of advantage to me;
And the earth's face upward for my inspection.

My feet are locked upon the rough bark.
It took the whole of Creation   10
To produce my foot, my each feather:
Now I hold Creation in my foot

Or fly up, and revolve it all slowly –
I kill where I please because it is all mine.

revolve it turn it round.

There is no sophistry in my body: 15
My manners are tearing off heads –

sophistry false reasoning, clever speeches.

The allotment of death.

allotment dealing out.

For the one path of my flight is direct
Through the bones of the living.
No arguments assert my right: 20

assert declare, establish.

The sun is behind me.
Nothing has changed since I began.
My eye has permitted no change.
I am going to keep things like this.

☆

Thinking/Talking Points

▷ Who is the speaker here?
   Do you think the *poet* agrees with everything the *speaker* says?

▷ Suggest half-a-dozen words to sum up the speaker's personality.
   What impressions of him does the phrase 'my eyes closed' suggest to you?

▷ Do you think the speaker has a 'falsifying dream'? If so, what is it?

▷ What does the speaker find 'convenient'?
   What does his attitude to these things tell us about him?
   Can you think of two meanings for 'The sun is behind me'?
   How is that remark typical of the speaker?

▷ Do you think there is any 'sophistry' in the speaker's arguments?

▷ Comment on the final line.

▷ Look again at the words you used to describe the speaker's personality.
   Are there any you wish to add or delete?

   Reread the poem carefully now to see what else deserves attention before you
   choose your assignment. Think about the tone of voice in which you would
   read the poem aloud.

Assignments

English

○ Compose a similar piece of thinking aloud for *one* of the following: a wasp;
   a dog; a lion; a tree; a mountain; a river; a cloud.

English Literature

○ What impression of the hawk and its outlook are we given in the poem?
   Do you find his view of himself and the world convincing?
   Refer closely to the text in your essay.

○ Would you agree that *Hawk Roosting* is a study of Power?
   What does it suggest about the way the powerful see the world? Does this
   speaker have any weaknesses?
   Remember to refer closely to the text in your answer.

Further reading

Oscar Wilde   *The Remarkable Rocket*

★

What comes to mind when you think about the months of September, October, and November?

What do you associate with Autumn rather than any other season? (Think about colours, smells and noises; weather; skyscapes; evenings; moods; work; games; clothes; food; animals; the countryside; city streets; school; plans; memories.)

If Autumn were a person, how old do you think he/she would be? What would he/she wear? What sort of person do you think she/he would be (e.g. calm; busy; noisy; cosy; decrepit; anxious; relaxed; stately; sluggish; timid; placid; subdued; scruffy; plump; skinny; motherly; friendly; brash; tender; lively; pompous; generous; mean; kind; cruel; rich; poor; wise; foolish; dreamy; sad; grumpy; happy; slow-moving)?
Add some words of your own.

Read through this poem carefully a few times. Give yourself time to think about the pictures it paints and the mood it suggests before considering the points which follow.

To Autumn

Season of mists and mellow fruitfulness,
   Close bosom-friend of the maturing sun,
Conspiring with him how to load and bless
   With fruit the vines that round the thatch-eaves run;
To bend with apples the moss'd cottage-trees   5
   And fill all fruit with ripeness to the core;
     To swell the gourd, and plump the hazel shells
   With a sweet kernel; to set budding more,
And still more, later flowers for the bees,
Until they think warm days will never cease,   10
     For Summer has o'er-brimm'd their clammy cells.

Who hath not seen thee oft amid thy store?
   Sometimes whoever seeks abroad may find
Thee sitting careless on a granary floor,
   Thy hair soft-lifted by the winnowing wind;   15
Or on a half-reap'd furrow sound asleep.
   Drows'd with the fume of poppies, while thy hook
     Spares the next swathe and all its twinèd flowers;
And sometimes like a gleaner thou dost keep
   Steady thy laden head across a brook;   20
   Or by a cider-press, with patient look,
     Thou watchest the last oozings hours by hours.

mellow *mature, ripe, rich, sweet, soft.*

conspiring *plotting.*

gourd *a large, fleshy fruit.*
kernel *soft inner part of a nut.*

o'er brimm'd *filled to overflowing.*
clammy *sticky.*

seeks abroad *looks around.*
granary *grain store.*
winnowing *separating the grain from the husks.*

drows'd *sent to sleep.*

swathe *line of cut corn.*

gleaner *someone who follows the reapers, gathering stray ears of corn.*
laden *loaded.*
cider-press *machine for crushing apples to make cider.*

Where are the songs of Spring? Ay, where are they?
　Think not of them, thou hast thy music too –
While barrèd clouds bloom the soft-dying day,　　　　　　24
　And touch the stubble-plains with rosy hue;
Then in a wailful choir, the small gnats mourn
　Among the river sallows, borne aloft
　　Or sinking as the light wind lives or dies;
And full-grown lambs loud bleat from hilly bourn;　　　　30
　Hedge-crickets sing; and now with treble soft
　The red-breast whistles from a garden-croft;
　　And gathering swallows twitter in the skies.

stubble-plains *fields which have been harvested.*
mourn *make a sad sound.*
sallows *willows.*

bourn *boundary, stream.*
treble *high-pitched song.*
garden-croft *allotment or vegetable patch.*

☆

Thinking/Talking Points

▷　Were your own ideas about Autumn like Keats's?
What was similar, what was different about the pictures and moods you thought of as 'autumnal'?

▷　Words have sounds which help to create a mood, and textures too. Just saying some words makes you feel alert or sleepy, edgy or relaxed. What feelings do the sounds and textures of these words give you: 'mists . . . mellow fruitfulness . . . maturing'?
See if you can find other words and phrases in the poem which work in a similar way.

▷　How do you think the poem should be read? Quickly or slowly? In a bright voice or a subdued one?
Do you think the poem would be better suited to a man's or a woman's voice?
How old would your ideal speaker be?

▷　Read lines 7–11 again to yourself.
What do you see, smell, taste, feel, hear as you read them?

▷　How would you describe the mood of stanza 2?
At what time of day do you imagine those scenes taking place?
The poet imagines Autumn as a person; we see him/her in three different settings.
Which of these three scenes do you like most?
See if you can imagine and describe a painting of that scene.

▷　What sounds are recalled in the last stanza?
Why do you think the gnats 'mourn'?
What is the effect of calling the sheep 'full-grown lambs'?
With which season do you associate crickets and red-breasts?
What do you feel as you read the final line?
See if you can explain why it has that effect.

Reread the poem now, two or three times, before you choose your assignment.

Assignments

English

○ Produce your own portrait of a season, of a month or of a special day in the year – in verse or in prose.
Think about colours, smells, sounds, moods . . .
Think about the weather and people's behaviour.
Try to imagine a person who is like the season or occasion.
See if, as Keats does, you can suggest something of the character of the moment through the tempo and the rhythm of your writing: e.g. long, lumbering, lethargic sentences . . . or quick, bright, sharp ones.

○ See if you can 'translate' Keats's poem into a drawing or painting or piece of music of your own.

English Literature

○ Essay: 'To evoke the season in words, Keats appeals to all our senses. The sounds and textures of the words he chooses are an important part of their "meaning".' Do you agree?
Examine the poem closely, describing the moods, the experiences of Autumn he shares with us, and looking at *how* the poem makes its appeal.
Which details did you particularly enjoy?

○ Essay: What picture of an Autumn day a century and a half ago do you imagine as you read Keats's poem?
Is your own experience of Autumn similar?
Remember to refer closely to the text in your essay.

★

Hardy
THE DARKLING THRUSH
and
NEUTRAL TONES

Assignments

1 *Late Afternoon in Winter*
Hard frost. No one about as you walk down a country lane.
A bird begins to sing.

○ With these details as a formula, write a piece of verse or prose to capture the experience, to share your feelings with the reader.
Decide upon a few graphic pieces of description to set the scene.
Where are you standing? What mood has the day? What are you thinking about? What kind of bird sings? How would you describe its song? How does that song echo/alter your mood on that cold evening?
If you write in verse, try to find a rhythm which is fitting for the moods you wish to convey.

2 *A Memory*
He recalls a winter's day and a girlfriend whose love had become as lifeless as the surroundings. There have been disappointments since.

○ Write a diary-reflection or a poem in which a man recalls the pain a woman caused him many years before, recalls the bleak countryside in which they parted as vividly as he remembers the pangs of a love dying.
What sort of day was it? Find a couple of descriptive details to capture the atmosphere.
What was she like? What were her feelings towards him/you?
How did he/you try to make conversation?
Decide upon one or two vividly recalled details to bring her before the reader's eyes, a phrase or two to capture the tone of that 'conversation'.
How did things work out after that? What still gives him/you pain after so many years?

When you have finished your own pieces and are satisfied with them, look at the poems below whose 'formulas' you have been writing to.

▷ How convincing were your descriptions of the situations?
▷ How would you describe the tone of each of these poems: the mood, the part the settings played?
▷ What similarities are there between what you wrote and what you find here?
▷ What are the biggest differences?
▷ Which of Hardy's lines do you wish you had written?

The Darkling Thrush

I leant upon a coppice gate
    When Frost was spectre-gray,
And Winter's dregs made desolate
    The weakening eye of day.
The tangle bine-stems scored the sky
    Like strings of broken lyres,
And all mankind that haunted nigh
    Had sought their household fires.

The land's sharp features seemed to be
    The Century's corpse outleant,
His crypt the cloudy canopy,
    The wind his death-lament.
The ancient pulse of germ and birth
    Was shrunken hard and dry,
And every spirit upon earth
    Seemed fervourless as I.

At once a voice arose among
    The bleak twigs overhead
In a full-hearted evensong
    Of joy illimited;
An aged thrush, frail, gaunt, and small,
    In blast-beruffled plume,
Had chosen thus to fling his soul
    Upon the growing gloom.

So little cause for carollings
    Of such ecstatic sound
Was written on terrestrial things
    Afar or nigh around,
That I could think there trembled through
    His happy good-night air
Some blessed Hope, whereof he knew
    And I was unaware.

☆

coppice wood of small trees.

spectre-gray ghostly gray.

dregs remains.
desolate uninhabited, bleak, dismal.

5 *bine-stems* dead stems of bindweed.
scored appeared to mark, scratch the sky as you looked up through them.
lyres an ancient kind of harp.

10 *haunted nigh* lived or worked nearby.
the Century's corpse the scene is set in the late 1890s.
outleant stretched out on the ground.
crypt burial-place.
cloudy canopy the sky.
15 *the ancient pulse of germ and birth* the spirit of generation, of growth.
fervourless unenthusiastic, miserable.

20 *illimited* unlimited.

frail weak.
gaunt lean, half-starved.
blast-beruffled plume feathers disordered, made untidy by the wind.

25 *carollings* cheerful songs.

terrestrial earthly.

nigh near.

30 *air* song.
whereof of which.

Neutral Tones

We stood by a pond that winter day,
And the sun was white, as though chidden of God,
And a few leaves lay on the starving sod;
    – They had fallen from an ash, and were gray.

Your eyes on me were as eyes that rove
Over tedious riddles of years ago;
And some words played between us to and fro
    On which lost the more by our love.

The smile on your mouth was the deadest thing
Alive enough to have strength to die;
And a grin of bitterness swept thereby
    Like an ominous bird a-wing . . .

Since then, keen lessons that love deceives,
And wrings with wrong, have shaped to me
Your face, and the God-curst sun, and a tree,
    And a pond edged with grayish leaves.

chidden scolded, rebuked.
starving sod dying, frozen ground.
ash a kind of tree.

5   *rove* wander.
tedious uninteresting, tiresome.

10

ominous warning of bad things to come.
keen sharp, painful.
shaped to me brought back to me the memory of.

15

☆

Assignments

English

○ See if you can write a series of winter poems which chronicle the dying of a love affair.

English Literature

○ Write a study of either or both of these poems, examining the details which you found particularly moving or effective in some way.

○ Choose one poem and the version of it which you wrote and discuss the ways in which the two poems are different. Which effects in your piece do you feel worked well; which bits need rethinking or rewriting? Are there any details in Hardy's poem which you feel were not very effective?

Further reading

Donne   *Nocturnall Upon S Lucies Day*
Muller   *Die Winterreise*
            (There is an English version in the *Penguin Book of Lieder* of this cycle of poems which were set to music by Schubert.)

★

Plath
WUTHERING HEIGHTS

Wuthering Heights is a novel by Emily Bronte, published in 1847.
It is a story of passionate love and hatred set in the wild Yorkshire moors.
'Wuthering Heights' is the house around which much of the action revolves.

What pictures, sounds, feelings do the words 'Wuthering Heights' suggest to you?
Make a guess at the meaning of 'wuthering'.
What sort of house do you picture?
What might you expect the mood of a poem called *Wuthering Heights* to be?

Read through the poem carefully two or three times before considering the points which follow.

Wuthering Heights

The horizons ring me like faggots,
Tilted and disparate, and always unstable.
Touched by a match, they might warm me,
And their fine lines singe
The air to orange   5
Before the distances they pin evaporate,
Weighting the pale sky with a solider color.
But they only dissolve and dissolve
Like a series of promises, as I step forward.

There is no life higher than the grasstops   10
Or the hearts of sheep, and the wind
Pours by like destiny, bending
Everything in one direction.
I can feel it trying
To funnel my heat away.   15
If I pay the roots of the heather
Too close attention, they will invite me
To whiten my bones among them.

The sheep know where they are,
Browsing in their dirty wool-clouds,   20
Gray as the weather.
The black slots of their pupils take me in.
It is like being mailed into space,
A thin, silly message.
They stand about in grandmotherly disguise,   25
All wig curls and yellow teeth
And hard, marbly baas.

faggots bundles of firewood.
tilted sloping.
disparate at odds with one another.
singe scorch.

pin mark.
weighting making heavier.
color colour.

destiny fate.

browsing grazing.

pupils opening in the iris of the eye.

I come to wheel ruts, and water
Limpid as the solitudes
That flee through my fingers.   30
Hollow doorsteps go from grass to grass;
Lintel and sill have unhinged themselves.
Of people the air only
Remembers a few odd syllables.
It rehearses them moaningly: 35
Black stone, black stone.

The sky leans on me, me, the one upright
Among all horizontals.
The grass is beating its head distractedly.
It is too delicate   40
For a life in such company;
Darkness terrifies it.
Now, in valleys narrow
And black as purses, the house lights
Gleam like small change.

limpid clear, transparent.
solitudes solitary places.

lintel and sill top and bottom of a window-frame.

horizontals lines parallel to the earth's surface.
distractedly wildly, madly, in a frenzy.

☆

Thinking/Talking Points

▷   How would you describe the mood of the poem?
    Which words and phrases particularly define the mood?
    Was it what you expected?

▷   Have you ever seen a picture in which somebody stood surrounded by faggots?
    How do you react to the idea 'Touched by a match, they might warm me'?
    Can you suggest reasons other than the weather for the speaker's feeling so
    cold?

▷   The speaker talks about a succession of horizons, 'Tilted and disparate'.
    Across what kind of countryside does this suggest she is walking?
    The final lines of stanza 1 compare the relentless dissolving of the horizons as
    she walks towards them to a situation she has experienced over and over again
    in her life.
    What do you think that situation has been?

▷   Read the second stanza again.
    Compare the description of the wind in the poem to this extract from Emily
    Bronte's novel:

    'Wuthering Heights' is the name of Mr Heathcliff's dwelling, *wuthering* being a
    significant provincial adjective, descriptive of the atmospheric tumult to which its
    station is exposed in stormy weather. Pure bracing ventilation they must have up there
    at all times, indeed: one may guess the power of the north wind, blowing over the edge,
    by the excessive slant of a few stunted firs at the end of the house; and by a range of
    gaunt thorns all stretching their limbs one way, as if craving alms of the sun.

▷ How would you describe the poet's attitude to the wind?
Why do you think she is afraid to stop and examine the roots of the heather?

▷ Look again at stanza 3.
How do you usually picture sheep?
Suggest half-a-dozen words or phrases to describe them.
How do you react to the way the speaker sees them?
What do you think she means by their 'grandmotherly disguise'?

▷ Look again at stanza 4.
How would you describe the speaker's situation here?
What is being imitated in the last line?

▷ Now read the final stanza again.
How does this idea make you feel: 'The sky leans on me'?
What is the mood of this passage:
'The grass is beating its head distractedly.
It is too delicate
For a life in such company.
Darkness terrifies it.'
How would you describe the mood of the final three lines of the poem?
What do you feel is responsible for the change?

▷ How do you imagine the eyes, the voice, the movements of the speaker at different moments in the poem?

Reread the poem now a couple of times to see what other points need thinking about before choosing your assignment.

Assignments

English

○ Write a poem or short story in which you explore your feelings, visiting a particular place at a particular time of year.

○ Draw or paint a picture suggested by the poem.

English Literature

○ Essay: Examine the changing moods of the speaker in *Wuthering Heights*.
How do you feel towards her?
Refer closely to the text in your answer.

Further reading

Plath	Poems	*Watercolour of Grantchester Meadows* (in *The Colossus*)
		I Am Vertical (in *Crossing the Water*)
Ted Hughes	Short story	*The Rain Horse* (in *Wodwo*)

★

ODE TO A NIGHTINGALE

Assignment

It is a clear, moonlit, summer's night. You are walking alone through a forest; there is no danger.

Suddenly, a nightingale releases a torrent of song into the darkness and you become aware of the heavy, rich scent of flowers.

Then the bird flies off, leaving you alone amongst the silent trees.

○ Jot down as many words and phrases as you can for each of the following:
   (a) the sensation of walking through a forest at night: the sounds, the smells, the touch of plants on your hands and face; the feeling of the ground beneath your feet;
   (b) the sound of the nightingale's song: what does it resemble? what memories does it stir? what feelings? how do you feel when the nightingale flies off?

How do you think such an experience would affect different people (e.g. someone in love, someone bereaved, someone about to leave the country)?

○ Write a short piece about the experience described in the first paragraph. Think about the sounds as well as the meanings of words.
   If you write in verse, think carefully about the *length of line* which would be most appropriate to the mood you wish to convey.

Read through the following poem carefully a few times before considering the points which follow.

Ode to a Nightingale

My heart aches, and a drowsy numbness pains
  My sense, as though of hemlock I had drunk,
Or emptied some dull opiate to the drains
  One minute past, and Lethe-wards had sunk;
'Tis not through envy of thy happy lot,   5
  But being too happy in thine happiness —
    That thou, light-wingèd Dryad of the trees,
      In some melodious plot
Of beechen green, and shadows numberless,
  Singest of summer in full-throated ease.   10

hemlock *a poison which slowly numbs the body towards death.*
opiate *a sleeping drug or painkiller.*
Lethe *the river in the Underworld whose waters make one forget everything.*
Dryad *a woodland spirit (here, the nightingale).*
beechen *amongst beech trees.*

O, for a draught of vintage! that hath been
　Cool'd a long age in the deep-delvèd earth,
Tasting of Flora and the country green,
　Dance, and Provençal song, and sunburnt mirth!
O for a beaker full of the warm South,　　　　　　　　15
　Full of the true, the blushful Hippocrene,
　　With beaded bubbles winking at the brim,
　　　And purple-stainèd mouth,
That I might drink, and leave the world unseen,
　And with thee fade away into the forest dim —　　　20

Fade far away, dissolve and quite forget
　What thou among the leaves hast never known,
The weariness, the fever, and the fret
　Here, where men sit and hear each other groan;
Where palsy shakes a few, sad, last gray hairs,　　　25
　Where youth grows pale, and spectre-thin, and dies;
　　Where but to think is to be full of sorrow
　　　And leaden-eyed despairs;
Where Beauty cannot keep her lustrous eyes,
　Or new Love pine at them beyond tomorrow.　　　　30

Away! away! for I will fly to thee,
　Not charioted by Bacchus and his pards,
But on the viewless wings of Poesy,
　Though the dull brain perplexes and retards.
Already with thee! tender is the night,　　　　　　　35
　And haply the Queen-Moon is on her throne,
　Cluster'd around by all her starry Fays;
　　　But here there is no light,
Save what from heaven is with the breezes blown
　Through verdurous glooms and winding mossy ways.　40

I cannot see what flowers are at my feet,
　Nor what soft incense hangs upon the boughs,
But, in embalmèd darkness, guess each sweet
　Wherewith the seasonable month endows
The grass, the thicket, and the fruit-tree wild;　　　45
　White hawthorn, and the pastoral eglantine;
　　Fast fading violets cover'd up in leaves;
　　　And mid-May's eldest child,
The coming musk-rose, full of dewy wine,
　The murmurous haunt of flies on summer eves.　　　50

---

a draught of vintage a glass of the best wine.
cool'd . . . in the deep-delvèd earth the wine has been buried deep in the ground.
Flora the goddess of flowers.
Provençal from Provence, a region of France famous for its wine.
Hippocrene a spring whose waters gave one the power of writing poetry.

palsy a disease of old age which makes the sufferer tremble uncontrollably.
spectre-thin thin as a ghost.

lustrous bright, beautiful, full of life.
pine yearn for, waste away.

Bacchus the god of wine.
pards the leopards who draw Bacchus's chariot.
viewless invisible.

Fays fairies, spirits.

verdurous lush, green.

embalmèd richly scented, spicy.
endows gives to.

pastoral eglantine wild honeysuckle (or sweet briar rose).

136

Darkling I listen; and, for many a time
   I have been half in love with easeful Death,
Call'd him soft names in many a musèd rhyme,
   To take into the air my quiet breath;
Now more than ever seems it rich to die,   *55*
   To cease upon the midnight with no pain,
      While thou art pouring forth thy soul abroad
         In such an ecstasy!
   Still wouldst thou sing, and I have ears in vain –
      To thy high requiem become a sod.   *60*

Thou wast not born for death, immortal Bird!
   No hungry generations tread thee down;
The voice I hear this passing night was heard
   In ancient days by emperor and clown:
Perhaps the self-same song that found a path   *65*
   Through the sad heart of Ruth, when, sick for home,
      She stood in tears amid the alien corn;
         The same that oft-times hath
   Charm'd magic casements, opening on the foam
      Of perilous seas, in faery lands forlorn.   *70*

Forlorn! the very word is like a bell
   To toll me back from thee to my sole self!
Adieu! the fancy cannot cheat so well
   As she is fam'd to do, deceiving elf,
Adieu! adieu! thy plaintive anthem fades   *75*
   Past the near meadows, over the still stream,
      Up the hill-side; and now 'tis buried deep
         In the next valley-glades;
   Was it a vision, or a waking dream?
      Fled is that music: Do I wake or sleep?

Glosses (right margin):

darkling *in the darkness.*

requiem *a hymn for the dead.*
sod *senseless turf.*

alien *foreign, unfamiliar.*

casements *windows.*

perilous *dangerous.*
forlorn *without hope, sad.*

toll *the chiming of a church bell (here, probably at a funeral).*
fancy *imagination.*
plaintive anthem *a mournful hymn.*

Thinking/Talking Points

▷ In the light of what you imagined, expected, wrote yourself, do you find the
opening of Keats's poem surprising?

▷ sad; quivering; fidget; loneliness; bicycle; gloom.
Which are the two longest words here?
Which two take the longest to say?
Think about the 'spoken length' of each of these words: painful; pattercake;
eel; elephant; pigeon; pie; rain; rippling; drowsy; ticket-collector; semiquaver;
sea; sentimental; lugubrious; happy; waiting; handicapped; easy; numb;
numbering; dividend; Lethe; lipstick; dry; mousetrap; bubbles; effervescent;
winning; wine . . .

▷ Which words in the first stanza do you find slow off the tongue?
Which are bright and lively?

137

How would you describe the speaker's mood in this stanza?
What do you think he can mean by 'being *too* happy in thine happiness'?
Can you recall a situation in which you were 'too happy'?

▷   What is the focus of attention in the second stanza?
What is it the speaker longs for?
Which words and images capture the appeal of wine?
What do these details suggest about the sort of person the speaker used to be?

▷   Look again at stanza 3.
What has led to the speaker's desire to 'fade . . . away'?
How does he picture old age? And youth?
What do you think has given him such an outlook?

▷   Look again at stanza 4.
In what senses is the brain 'dull'?
What *kind* of thinking enables the poet for a moment to 'join' the bird?
How is the experience of the world the poet now enjoys (lines 35–50) different
from the way he saw the world in stanza 3?
How does he make *us* feel the pleasures he is describing?

▷   Read stanzas 6 and 7 again.
What does the speaker see as the difference between the nightingale and
himself?
Can you think of a way in which they are more similar than he realises?

▷   'forlorn . . . Forlorn' (lines 70–71).
What sound does the word imitate?
Why do you think the speaker now calls fancy (imagination) a 'deceiving elf'?

▷   What is happening to the nightingale's song as the poem ends?
What mood do you think the speaker is in when he leaves us?

Reread the poem carefully now two or three times to see what else deserves
attention before you choose your assignment.

Assignments

English

○   *Joy and Pain*
Write a piece of poetry or prose in which the experience of seeing or hearing
something beautiful makes the speaker thoughtful, nostalgic, downcast . . .
(e.g. an old person watching children play; a broken-hearted lover at a
firework display or at a concert; a widow(er) walking along the seashore;
a handicapped person sitting in the park; a dying person watching the sunset).

English Literature

○   Essay: How would you describe the speaker's feelings at different points in *Ode
to a Nightingale*?
Examine the ways in which Keats conveys a complex mood of pleasure mixed
with pain, ecstasy mixed with despair.
Do you understand the speaker's feelings? Do you find the poem moving?
Give your reasons. Remember to refer closely to the text in your answer.

★

= Plath =
TULIPS

What happens to a *person* when he/she becomes a hospital *patient*?
Why do you think some people make very bad patients?

Why do visitors often take flowers to patients in hospital?
Of what things are they reminders?
What sentiments might they express?
How would you expect someone you loved to react to such a present?

Read through the following poem carefully three or four times and give
yourself time to think about the attitude of the speaker before considering the
points which follow.

Tulips

The tulips are too excitable, it is winter here.
Look how white everything is, how quiet, how snowed-in.
I am learning peacefulness, lying by myself quietly
As the light lies on these white walls, this bed, these hands.
I am nobody; I have nothing to do with explosions.   5
I have given my name and my day-clothes up to the nurses
And my history to the anesthetist and my body to surgeons.

    anesthetist *the American
    spelling of anaesthetist.*

They have propped my head between the pillow and the
                                     sheet-cuff
Like an eye between two white lids that will not shut.
Stupid pupil, it has to take everything in.   10
The nurses pass and pass, they are no trouble,
They pass the way gulls pass inland in their white caps,
Doing things with their hands, one just the same as another,
So it is impossible to tell how many there are.

My body is a pebble to them, they tend it as water   15
Tends to the pebbles it must run over, smoothing them gently.
They bring me numbness in their bright needles, they bring me
                                     sleep.
Now I have lost myself I am sick of baggage –
My patent leather overnight case like a black pillbox,
My husband and child smiling out of the family photo;   20
Their smiles catch onto my skin, little smiling hooks.

I have let things slip, a thirty-year-old cargo boat
Stubbornly hanging on to my name and address.
They have swabbed me clear of my loving associations.
Scared and bare on the green plastic-pillowed trolley   25
I watched my teaset, my bureaus of linen, my books
Sink out of sight, and the water went over my head.
I am a nun now, I have never been so pure.

I didn't want any flowers, I only wanted
To lie with my hands turned up and be utterly empty.   30
How free it is, you have no idea how free –
The peacefulness is so big it dazes you,
And it asks nothing, a name tag, a few trinkets.   *trinkets* keepsakes.
It is what the dead close on, finally; I imagine them
Shutting their mouths on it, like a Communion tablet.   35   ***a Communion tablet*** *wafer taken at Holy Communion.*

The tulips are too red in the first place, they hurt me.
Even through the gift paper I could hear them breathe
Lightly, through their white swaddlings, like an awful baby. ***swaddlings*** *(literally) clothes in which babies used to be tightly wrapped.*
Their redness talks to my wound, it corresponds.
They are subtle: they seem to float, though they weigh me
                                               down,   40
Upsetting me with their sudden tongues and their color,
A dozen red lead sinkers round my neck.   ***sinkers*** *weights fixed to something to make it sink.*

Nobody watched me before, now I am watched.
The tulips turn to me, and the window behind me
Where once a day the light slowly widens and slowly thins,   45
And I see myself, flat, ridiculous, a cut-paper shadow
Between the eye of the sun and the eyes of the tulips,
And I have no face, I have wanted to efface myself.   *efface wipe out, withdraw.*
The vivid tulips eat my oxygen.

Before they came the air was calm enough,   50
Coming and going, breath by breath, without any fuss.
Then the tulips filled it up like a loud noise.
Now the air snags and eddies round them the way a river   ***snags and eddies*** *gets caught and swirls around.*
Snags and eddies round a sunken rust-red engine.
They concentrate my attention, that was happy   55
Playing and resting without committing itself.

The walls, also, seem to be warming themselves.
The tulips should be behind bars like dangerous animals;
They are opening like the mouth of some great African cat,
And I am aware of my heart: it opens and closes   60
Its bowl of red blooms out of sheer love of me.
The water I taste is warm and salt, like the sea,
And comes from a country far away as health.

☆

Thinking/Talking Points

▷ How would you describe the speaker's mood in the opening lines of the poem? From what she says later, why do you think she resents the flowers so much? (What things do they remind her of? What claims, what demands does she feel the gift makes?)
Have you ever had similar feelings about a present?

▷ '. . . it is winter here.'
Which descriptive details develop this idea of the hospital?
Which details suggest that her mind is in a kind of hibernation?

▷ '. . . the light lies on these white walls, this bed, these hands.'
What is the effect of the speaker including her hands in the list?
How would you describe her attitude to her body?

▷ Were you surprised by the list of 'baggage' in stanza 3?
Why do you think she regards her family's smiles as 'little . . . hooks'?

▷ 'I am a nun now, I have never been so pure.'
What exactly do you think the speaker means here by 'pure'?
Do you think she is like a nun?

▷ When does someone 'lie with' their 'hands turned up'?
Can you suggest what the speaker wants?

▷ Read lines 36–43 again.
What do you make of the way the flowers are described?
Can you explain in your own words how the speaker feels towards them?

▷ How would you describe the tone, the mood of the final lines?
What effect does the arrival of the tulips appear to be having?

Reread the poem two or three times to see what other details deserve attention before you choose an assignment. You may like to think about how you would read the poem aloud: at what pace, at what volume, in what tone of voice.

Assignments

English

○ *The Visit*
See if you can tell the story, from the point of view of the patient's husband or child, of the visit when those tulips were presented.
You may like to write entirely in dialogue or entirely as the narrator's unspoken thoughts.

○ You are the consultant looking after this patient. As a series of case-notes, describe her gradually improving state of health.

English Literature

○ Essay: 'A disturbing insight into a mind horribly clear in its desire for extinction.' With close reference to the text, discuss how adequate you find this description of *Tulips*.
Are you able to identify with the speaker?

★

== Tennyson ==
ULYSSES

Ulysses (also known as Odysseus) was the hero of Homer's epic poem *The Odyssey*. After playing a major role in the Greeks' victory over the Trojans, Ulysses endured many hardships and trials of his courage and strength in the perilous journey back to Ithaca, his kingdom. There, after ridding the court of the suitors who had beseiged her, he was reunited with his faithful wife, Penelope, and their son, Telemachus.

In this monologue, the epic hero, now in his old age, thinks about his family and his kingdom and about what life still has to offer him. Read it through carefully two or three times before thinking about the points which follow.

Ulysses

It little profits that an idle king,
By this still hearth, among these barren crags,
Match'd with an aged wife, I mete and dole
Unequal laws unto a savage race,
That hoard, and sleep, and feed, and know not me.   5
I cannot rest from travel: I will drink
Life to the lees: all times I have enjoy'd
Greatly, have suffer'd greatly, both with those
That loved me, and alone; on shore, and when
Thro' scudding drifts the rainy Hyades   10
Vext the dim sea: I am become a name;
For always roaming with a hungry heart
Much have I seen and known; cities of men
And manners, climates, councils, governments,
Myself not least, but honour'd of them all;   15
And drunk delight of battle with my peers,
Far on the ringing plains of windy Troy.
I am a part of all that I have met;
Yet all experience is an arch wherethro'
Gleams that untravell'd world, whose margin fades   20
For ever and for ever when I move.
How dull it is to pause, to make an end,
To rust unburnish'd, not to shine in use!
As tho' to breathe were life. Life piled on life
Were all too little, and of one to me   25
Little remains: but every hour is saved
From that eternal silence, something more,
A bringer of new things; and vile it were

it little profits it's hardly worth while or satisfying.
barren crags bare, rough rocks.
mete and dole measure and deal out (justice).
hoard gather and hide away (money, valuables . . .)
to the lees to the dregs.

scudding drifts waves whipped up by the wind.
Hyades a constellation of stars associated with bad weather.
vext angered.

peers equals.

margin border.

unburnish'd unpolished.

For some three suns to store and hoard myself,
And this grey spirit yearning in desire   30
To follow knowledge, like a sinking star,
Beyond the utmost bound of human thought.
　This is my son, mine own Telemachus,
To whom I leave the sceptre and the isle –
Well-loved of me, discerning to fulfil   35
This labour, by slow prudence to make mild
A rugged people, and thro' soft degrees
Subdue them to the useful and the good.
Most blameless is he, centred in the sphere
Of common duties, decent not to fail   40
In offices of tenderness, and pay
Meet adoration to my household gods,
When I am gone. He works his work, I mine.
　There lies the port: the vessel puffs her sail:
There gloom the dark broad seas. My mariners,   45
Souls that have toil'd, and wrought, and thought with me –
That ever with a frolic welcome took
The thunder and the sunshine, and opposed
Free hearts, free foreheads – you and I are old;
Old age hath yet his honour and his toil;   50
Death closes all: but something ere the end,
Some work of noble note, may yet be done,
Not unbecoming men that strove with Gods.
The lights begin to twinkle from the rocks:
The long day wanes: the slow moon climbs: the deep   55
Moans round with many voices. Come, my friends,
'Tis not too late to seek a newer world.
Push off, and sitting well in order smite
The sounding furrows; for my purpose holds
To sail beyond the sunset, and the baths   60
Of all the western stars, until I die.
It may be that the gulfs will wash us down:
It may be we shall touch the Happy Isles,
And see the great Achilles, whom we knew.
Tho' much is taken, much abides; and tho'   65
We are not now that strength which in old days
Moved earth and heaven; that which we are, we are;
One equal temper of heroic hearts,
Made weak by time and fate, but strong in will
To strive, to seek, to find, and not to yield.

sceptre *staff, a symbol of kingship.*
discerning *shrewd, clear-sighted.*
prudence *being cautious, not taking risks.*

meet adoration *appropriate worship.*

mariners *sailors.*
toil'd, and wrought *worked hard.*
frolic *light-hearted, cheerful.*

not unbecoming *suiting, appropriate for.*
strove *struggled, wrestled.*
wanes *fades away.*
the deep *the ocean.*

smite the sounding furrows *strike (with oars) the roaring waves.*

gulfs *whirlpools.*

Achilles *another Greek hero.*
abides *remains.*

temper *temperament.*

yield *give in.*

☆

Thinking/Talking Points

▷ What is your impression of Ulysses?
What do you think he looks like?
How do you imagine his eyes? His hands?
What kind of voice do you hear?
Which phrases capture his attitude to physical hardships?

▷ 'I cannot rest from travel: I will drink
Life to the lees . . .'
Which other phrases capture the old hero's enthusiasm, his willingness to take risks?

▷ What do these lines suggest about the king's feelings towards his people:
'a savage race,
That hoard, and sleep, and feed . . .'
What is lacking from their lives?
In what sense(s) do they 'not know' Ulysses?

▷ 'I am become a name.'
What do you suppose Ulysses means by it?
Would you regard that as a great achievement, a burden or a failure?

▷ Which phrases tell us most about Ulysses's attitude to war?
What pictures do his memories of Troy suggest to you?

▷ What do you think Ulysses means when he says:
'I am a part of all that I have met.'

▷ Look again at lines 19–23.
How would you describe Ulysses's attitude to past achievements?
'As tho' to breathe were life.'
What do you think is the difference between *existing* and *living*?

▷ Look again at lines 33–43.
What can you deduce about Ulysses's relationship with his son, Telemachus?
Is he the sort of son Ulysses hoped for?
Suggest three or four words of your own to describe Telemachus's personality and outlook on life.
In what tone of voice would you read:
'He works his work, I mine'?

▷ Who do you think Ulysses feels closest to: his mariners, his people, his wife or his son? Can you explain why?

▷ How would you express in your own words Ulysses's decision at the end of the poem?
What expression do you see in his face?

Reread the poem carefully now to see what else deserves attention before you choose your assignment.

Assignments

English

- *Lost But Not Forgotten*
  A month later, Ulysses and all his crew are lost at sea. His son, Telemachus, is asked by a reporter for an assessment of his father's achievements and personality. Using details from the poem but adding plenty of your own ideas, write the interview.

- Imagine a crisis at sea: a pirate attack, a typhoon, a shipwreck, a mutiny . . . From the point of view of one of his crew, write a story about such an emergency and how Ulysses handles the situation, keeps up his men's spirits, sees them through.

- When Ulysses was much younger, a terrible prophecy was made to him. As a punishment for his blinding the Cyclops (a one-eyed giant) he would one day find himself wandering in a distant country, so far from the sea that the inhabitants ate unsalted food, knew nothing about boats and mistook the oar which the wanderer was carrying for a winnowing fan.
  Imagine yourself as Ulysses at such a time, in such a place, surrounded by such foreigners. See if you can compose a monologue, in verse or prose, exploring his thoughts.

English Literature

- Essay: 'Tennyson's *Ulysses*'.
  A later poet said 'Old men ought to be explorers'. What do you think he meant by that?
  Do you think he would have approved of the Ulysses who speaks in this poem? What would be your own assessment of Ulysses's character?

- With close reference to the text show how Tennyson explores the present situation of the old man.

Further study

- Eliot's poem *Gerontion* could be regarded as a parody (but not a comic one) of Tennyson's poem. You may like to compare and contrast the situations and outlooks of the two characters.

★

Eliot
THE LOVE SONG
OF J. ALFRED PRUFROCK

In his poem *The Shepherd* Hopkins contrasts the heroic sufferings of Christ
'fronting forked lightning . . .
  The horror and the havoc and the glory . . .'
with ordinary people's tame tempests and fussy fevers. Hopkins sums up the
triviality of his own existence with this striking image:
  'I . . . in smooth spoons spy life's masque mirrored.'
What does the image make you see?

What do you understand by the word 'hero'?
Do you think that where and when one lives determines one's chances of being
a hero? (e.g. Do you think somebody could be heroic at a cocktail party or
working in a supermarket, sitting in a launderette or watching television?)

Are you the heroic type?
Who are your heroes?
See if you can come up with a formula for a hero.
What might be the landmarks in a hero's life?

What do you suppose an 'anti-hero' is?
Can you think of one? What makes him/her unheroic?
What might be a good name for an anti-hero?
What might he/she look like? How might he/she behave?
How do you imagine his/her private thoughts?

Assignment

English

○ Consider this passage from Dickens's *Hard Times* and then suggest a programme
for an anti-hero's day.

It was a town of red brick, or of brick that would have been red if the smoke and ashes
had allowed it; but as matters stood it was a town of unnatural red and black like the
painted face of a savage. It was a town of machinery and tall chimneys, out of which
interminable serpents of smoke trailed themselves for ever and ever, and never got
uncoiled. It had a black canal in it, and a river that ran purple with ill-smelling dye, and
vast piles of buildings full of windows where there was a rattling and a trembling all day
long, and where the piston of the steam-engine worked monotonously up and down
like the head of an elephant in a state of melancholy madness. It contained several large
streets all very like one another, and many small streets still more like one another,
inhabited by people equally like one another, who all went in and out at the same
hours, with the same sound upon the same pavements, to do the same work, and to
whom every day was the same as yesterday and tomorrow, and every year the
counterpart of the last and the next.

Before you work on the following poem, look again at Marvell's *To His Coy Mistress* on pages 53–54.
Do you think there is anything heroic about Marvell's speaker?
The Love Song of J. Alfred Prufrock includes some echoes of Marvell's poem; you could regard it as a modern parody of *To His Coy Mistress*.

Remind yourself of the themes and mood of *To His Coy Mistress* and then read through Eliot's poem three or four times before considering the points which follow.

The Love Song of J. Alfred Prufrock

S'io credessi che mia riposta fosse,
A persona che mai tornasse al mondo,
Questa fiamma staria senza piu scosse,
Ma per ciò che giammai di questo fondo,
Non tornò viva alcun, s'i'odo il vero,
Senza tema d'infamia ti rispondo.

Let us go then, you and I,
When the evening is spread out against the sky
Like a patient etherised upon a table;   *etherised* under anaesthetic.
Let us go, through certain half-deserted streets,
The muttering retreats   *5*
Of restless nights in one-night cheap hotels
And sawdust restaurants with oyster-shells:
Streets that follow like a tedious argument
Of insidious intent   *of insidious intent* with hidden motives.
To lead you to an overwhelming question . . .   *10*
Oh, do not ask, 'What is it?'
Let us go and make our visit.

In the room the women come and go
Talking of Michelangelo   *Michelangelo* the greatest sculptor of the Renaissance.

The yellow fog that rubs its back upon the window-panes,   *15*
The yellow smoke that rubs its muzzle on the window-panes
Licked its tongue into the corners of the evening,
Lingered upon the pools that stand in drains,
Let fall upon its back the soot that falls from chimneys,
Slipped by the terrace, made a sudden leap,   *20*
And seeing that it was a soft October night,
Curled once about the house, and fell asleep.

And indeed there will be time
For the yellow smoke that slides along the street
Rubbing its back upon the window-panes;   *25*
There will be time, there will be time
To prepare a face to meet the faces that you meet;
There will be time to murder and create,
And time for all the works and days of hands
That lift and drop a question on your plate;   *30*

Time for you and time for me,
And time yet for a hundred indecisions,
And for a hundred visions and revisions,
Before the taking of a toast and tea.

In the room the women come and go   *35*
Talking of Michelangelo.

And indeed there will be time
To wonder, 'Do I dare?' and 'Do I dare?'
Time to turn back and descend the stair,
With a bald spot in the middle of my hair –   *40*
(They will say: 'How his hair is growing thin!')
My morning coat, my collar mounting firmly to the chin,
My necktie rich and modest, but asserted by a simple pin –
(They will say: 'But how his arms and legs are thin!')
Do I dare   *45*
Disturb the universe?
In a minute there is time
For decisions and revisions which a minute will reverse.

For I have known them all already, known them all –
Have known the evenings, mornings, afternoons,   *50*
I have measured out my life with coffee spoons;
I know the voices dying with a dying fall
Beneath the music from a farther room.
So how should I presume?

And I have known the eyes already, known them all –   *55*
The eyes that fix you in a formulated phrase,   **formulated phrase** *cliché*
And when I am formulated, sprawling on a pin,   *or epigram.*
When I am pinned and wriggling on the wall,
Then how should I begin
To spit out all the butt-ends of my days and ways?   *60*   **butt-ends** *cigarette-ends.*
And how should I presume?

And I have known the arms already, known them all –
Arms that are braceleted and white and bare
(But in the lamplight, downed with light brown hair!)
Is it perfume from a dress   *65*
That makes me so digress?   **digress** *wander off the*
Arms that lie along a table, or wrap about a shawl.   *subject.*
And should I then presume?
And how should I begin?   **presume** *dare to make the*
                                                                attempt.

          ·   ·   ·   ·   ·

Shall I say, I have gone at dusk through narrow streets   *70*
And watched the smoke that rises from the pipes
Of lonely men in shirt-sleeves, leaning out of windows?

I should have been a pair of ragged claws   **scuttling** *scurrying,*
Scuttling across the floors of silent seas.   *running away.*

          ·   ·   ·   ·   ·

148

And the afternoon, the evening, sleeps so peacefully! 75
Smoothed by long fingers,
Asleep . . . tired . . . or it malingers,
Stretched on the floor, here beside you and me.
Should I, after tea and cakes and ices,
Have the strength to force the moment to its crisis? 80
But though I have wept and fasted, wept and prayed,
Though I have seen my head (grown slightly bald) brought in
                                        upon a platter,
I am no prophet – and here's no great matter;
I have seen the moment of my greatness flicker,
And I have seen the eternal Footman hold my coat, and snicker, 85
And in short, I was afraid.

    And would it have been worth it, after all,
After the cups, the marmalade, the tea,
Among the porcelain, among some talk of you and me,
Would it have been worth while, 90
To have bitten off the matter with a smile,
To have squeezed the universe into a ball
To roll it towards some overwhelming question,
To say: 'I am Lazarus, come from the dead,
Come back to tell you all, I shall tell you all' – 95
If one, settling a pillow by her head,
    Should say: 'That is not what I meant at all.
    That is not it, at all.'

    And would it have been worth it, after all,
Would it have been worth while, 100
After the sunsets and the dooryards and the sprinkled streets,
After the novels, after the teacups, after the skirts that trail
                                        along the floor –
And this, and so much more? –
It is impossible to say just what I mean!
But as if a magic lantern threw the nerves in patterns on a
                                        screen: 105
Would it have been worth while
If one, settling a pillow or throwing off a shawl,
And turning towards the window, should say:
    'That it is not it at all,
    That is not what I meant, at all.' 110
                . . . . . .

    No! I am not Prince Hamlet, nor was meant to be;
Am an attendant lord, one that will do
To swell a progress, start a scene or two,
Advise the prince; no doubt, an easy tool,
Deferential, glad to be of use, 115
Politic, cautious, and meticulous;
Full of high sentence, but a bit obtuse;
At times, indeed, almost ridiculous –
Almost, at times, the Fool.

---

malingers *pretends to be ill to avoid doing something.*

platter *plate or dish.*

snicker *snigger.*

porcelain *delicate, expensive china.*

Lazarus *the poor beggar in Christ's parable (Luke 16). Dives, the rich man sent to Hell for his greed, begs that Lazarus be allowed to return from the dead to warn Dives's brothers that they must mend their ways or suffer his fate. Prufrock flirts with the idea of lecturing those around him about their moral failings.*

magic lantern *projector.*

Prince Hamlet *the hero of Shakespeare's play.*

deferential *polite, knowing one's place; also someone who endlessly puts things off.*
the Fool *the wise jester in Shakespeare's King Lear.*

I grow old . . . I grow old . . .   120
I shall wear the bottoms of my trousers rolled.

*the bottoms of my
trousers rolled i.e. in the
latest fashion.*

   Shall I part my hair behind? Do I dare to eat a peach?
I shall wear white flannel trousers, and walk upon the beach.
I have heard the mermaids singing, each to each.

I do not think that they will sing to me.   125

I have seen them riding seaward on the waves
Combing the white hair of the waves blown back
When the wind blows the water white and black.

We have lingered in the chambers of the sea
By sea-girls wreathed with seaweed red and brown   130
Till human voices wake us, and we drown.

Note: The words of the epigraph, 'S'io credessi . . . ti rispondo' come from
Dante's poem about Hell, *The Inferno*. The words are spoken by Guido, a
prisoner of Hell. Freely translated, they read, 'If I thought you would repeat
my story to a living soul, I should remain silent. But since no-one ever
leaves this place, I will tell you the truth about myself without fear of
shame.'
As you work through the poem, think about how far Prufrock's situation
resembles Guido's.

☆

Thinking/Talking Points

▷   What did you *expect* of this character, simply from his name?
    Guess his profession.
    What sort of family do you think he comes from?
    How does he speak?
    What sort of haircut, what sort of shoes, what sort of hobbies do you imagine
    Prufrock has?

▷   Based on your initial impressions of him, choose from this list a dozen or so
    words and phrases to describe Prufrock's personality:
    bold; staid; shy; vacillating; easily embarrassed; thick-skinned; intelligent;
    lazy; anxious; wild; pompous; charismatic; a snob; sensitive; a poseur; a rebel;
    brave; self-centred; morose; cowardly; gregarious; a dreamer; inhibited;
    reliable; manly; solitary; amusing; confused; foolish; dangerous; self-
    conscious; typical; sad.
    Add some words of your own to those you choose.

▷   How would you describe the 'world' Prufrock lives in? (With what sort(s) of
    people does he most often come into contact? What can you deduce from the
    poem about (a) his attitude to them? (b) their attitude to him?)

▷   Look again at the beginning of the poem.
    The poem starts as a love-song might. When does that mood break?

▷   What do you make of the simile
    'Like a patient etherised upon a table'?

Do you think it is an appropriate simile
(a) to describe an evening
(b) for *Prufrock* to choose?

▷ Prufrock tries to get the love-song off on its tracks again in line 4 but the sights and atmosphere of the down-town area of the place where he lives somehow get in the way.
What impression of the town do lines 4−9 give you?
What do you think Prufrock feels about the area? (Think what he means by 'muttering . . . restless . . . tedious argument
Of insidious intent
To lead you to an overwhelming question . . .'.)

▷ What do you suppose the 'overwhelming question' might be?
Why would it 'overwhelm' him?

▷ 'Oh, do not ask, "What is it?"
Let us go and make our visit.'
(a) Was that how you expected the sentence 'Let us go . . .' to end?
(b) This is one of the ghastliest rhymes in English poetry. Why do you think Eliot wrote it? Can you find the even ghastlier one which comes later in the poem?

▷ Look at lines 13−14 again.
What sort of women do you imagine? What sort of talk?
Why do you think Eliot repeats this couplet, unchanged, later?
How do you think Prufrock feels whilst this talk is going on?

▷ Look at lines 15−22.
The fog seems to have a life and character of its own. What animal do its movements suggest?
'Curled once about the house, and fell asleep.'
Does that remind you of an earlier line?

▷ Look again at lines 23−34.
It's as if Prufrock is having an argument with himself.
How could the passage be rewritten for two voices?

▷ 'And indeed there will be time . . .'
What does Prufrock do with his time? (Remember the speaker in Marvell's poem.)
Why do you think routines are so much a part of Prufrock's life?

▷ Why do you suppose Prufrock is preoccupied with his appearance?
How does he dress? Why doesn't that give him confidence?

▷ Look again at lines 49−69.
What do these lines tell us about Prufrock's position in the society in which he moves? How does he feel 'in company'?
Which phrases reveal that he is aware of the falsity and snobbery?

▷ Of what *feelings* in particular is Prufrock most nervous?
Why do you think he doesn't *know* how to begin?

▷ In lines 70−72, it's as if Prufrock attempts again to begin his love song, this time in the latest style.
What happens to the attempt?

▷ Read lines 79–84 again.
Why that awful rhyming couplet?
Do you know whose head was 'brought in upon a platter'?
Is Prufrock in *any* sense like a prophet? (Think of 'visions . . . revisions'.)

▷ What picture do you see here (lines 84–86):
'I have seen the moment of my greatness flicker'?
Who do you think 'the eternal Footman' is? (How do you imagine him looking at Prufrock? What sort of coat might he be holding? What 'overwhelming question' might he ask Prufrock or any of us?)

▷ In the lines we have just looked at, Prufrock comes close to seeing himself clearly. Perhaps that fear could have released him from the living Hell he creates for himself. (In one of Eliot's plays someone says 'Hell is oneself'.)
Why do you think, immediately after that moment of honesty, Prufrock lapses into his old social and mental habits?

Reread the rest of the poem a couple of times before considering the remaining points.

▷ What do you think Prufrock is trying to convince himself about in lines 92–97?
What sequel to these lines might we expect?
How would you describe the way the woman actually responds?

▷ 'I am no prophet . . . I am not Prince Hamlet . . .'
Do you think Prufrock is being modest here?
What happens to the train of thought in lines 111–119?

▷ 'I grow old . . . I grow old . . .'
What kind of thought might we expect to follow those words?
See if you can write an alternative second line to the couplet.

▷ Early in the poem Prufrock asks:
'Do I dare disturb the universe? . . .'
Towards the end he wonders
'Do I dare to eat a peach?'
What does setting those two questions alongside one another reveal about the way Prufrock's mind works?

▷ What is the one definite decision Prufrock makes in the course of the poem?
How would you describe Prufrock's state of mind in lines 120–123?

▷ What is the effect of the sudden shift from Prufrock's narrative to
'*We* have . . .
Till human voices wake *us* . . .' at the end of the poem?
What do you think Eliot is suggesting about Prufrock's situation?
Do you feel you are like Prufrock in any way?

▷ The epigraph (*S'io credessi . . .*) comes from Dante's vision of Hell. The speaker confesses the truth about himself, confident that his words will never be known to a living soul.
To what extent is Prufrock's confession like that?
Why do you think he can't admit the truth, most of the time even to himself?

Reread the poem a couple of times and give yourself plenty of time to think about it before you choose your assignment.

Assignments

English

○ *The Prisoner*
Write a 'confession' along similar lines, in verse or prose, in which the speaker describes the routines, rules and pressures which govern his life and from which she/he cannot escape, except occasionally in dreams.
Try to bring out the tension the speaker feels in 'keeping up appearances', making everyone believe that there are no anxieties, frustrations, longings.

English Literature

○ Write J. Alfred Prufrock's obituary, done by a society journalist.

○ Draw some pictures of Prufrock in his world.

○ Essay: 'I have measured out my life with coffee spoons'.
How appropriate an epitaph upon Prufrock do you think this would be? What has been the function of routine in his life? To what extent do you think his plight is a common one?

○ Essay: With close reference to the texts, compare and contrast Marvell's *To His Coy Mistress* and Eliot's *The Love Song of J. Alfred Prufrock*.
Do you feel both poems have important things to say?
With which do you feel more in tune?

○ Essay: 'Prufrock is a twentieth-century Hamlet – a thinking, anxious, self-conscious, paralysed man. He can think only who he is *not* like; he has no identity of his own. In Prufrock we see ourselves.' Do you agree?
Refer closely to the text in your answer.

○ Give a reading of the poem.

★

=== Tennyson ===
TITHONUS

If the Gods granted you just one wish what would it be?
In literature, such requests have had a habit of back-firing.
Can you think of penalties which might come with the following gifts: X-ray vision; the ability to fly; supersensitive hearing; massive strength; remarkable beauty; extraordinary intelligence; unlimited wealth; invisibility; your own chocolate factory.

The speaker of the following lines, Tithonus, asked to live for ever.
Would you feel confident about asking for such a gift?
What do you think you would gain, would lose, by ceasing to be a mere human?

Read through the poem carefully two or three times before thinking about the points which follow.

Tithonus

The woods decay, the woods decay and fall,
The vapours weep their burthen to the ground,
Man comes and tills the field and lies beneath,
And after many a summer dies the swan.
Me only cruel immortality   *5*
Consumes: I wither slowly in thine arms,
Here at the quiet limit of the world,
A white-hair'd shadow roaming like a dream
The ever-silent spaces of the East,
Far-folded mists, and gleaming halls of morn.   *10*

   Alas! for this grey shadow, once a man –
So glorious in his beauty and thy choice,
Who madest him thy chosen, that he seem'd
To his great heart none other than a God!
I ask'd thee, 'Give me immortality'.   *15*
Then didst thou grant mine asking with a smile,
Like wealthy men who care not how they give.
But thy strong Hours indignant work'd their wills,
And beat me down and marr'd and wasted me,
And tho' they could not end me, left me maim'd   *20*
To dwell in presence of immortal youth,
Immortal age beside immortal youth,
And all I was, in ashes. Can thy love,
Thy beauty, make amends, tho' even now,
Close over us, the silver star, thy guide,   *25*
Shines in those tremulous eyes that fill with tears
To hear me? Let me go: take back thy gift:

vapours mists.
weep their burthen to the ground the poet is comparing rain to tears.
tills cultivates.
immortality eternal life.
consumes destroys, eats up.
wither grow feebler, shrivel up.
limit boundary.
roaming wandering.
morn morning.

indignant resentfully.
worked their wills had their own way.
marr'd spoiled.
wasted me took away my strength.
end kill.
maim'd crippled, mutilated.
dwell live.
make amends repay, compensate for.
the silver star the morning star.
tremulous unsteady.

154

Why should a man desire in any way
To vary from the kindly race of men,   **kindly** *customary.*
Or pass beyond the goal of ordinance   30   **the goal of ordinance** *the*
Where all should pause, as is most meet for all?   *limit (of human life) which*
                                                        has been laid down.
                                                        meet *proper, appropriate.*

    A soft air fans the cloud apart; there comes
A glimpse of that dark world where I was born.
Once more the old mysterious glimmer steals
From thy pure brows, and from thy shoulders pure, 35
And bosom beating with a heart renew'd.
Thy cheek begins to redden thro' the gloom,
Thy sweet eyes brighten slowly close to mine,
Ere yet they blind the stars, and the wild team   **the wild team** *i.e. of*
Which love thee, yearning for thy yoke, arise,   40 *horses.*
And shake the darkness from their loosen'd manes,   **yoke** *harness, control.*
And beat the twilight into flakes of fire.
    Lo! ever thus thou growest beautiful
In silence, then before thine answer given
Departest, and thy tears are on my cheek.   45

    Why wilt thou ever scare me with thy tears,
And make me tremble lest a saying learnt
In days far-off, on that dark earth, be true?
'The Gods themselves cannot recall their gifts.'
    Ay me! ay me! with what another heart   50
In days far-off, and with what other eyes
I used to watch – if I be he that watch'd –
The lucid outline forming round thee; saw   **lucid** *clear, bright.*
The dim curls kindle into sunny rings;   **kindle** *catch fire, brighten.*
Changed with thy mystic change, and felt my blood 55 **mystic** *mysterious, magical.*
Glow with the glow that slowly crimson'd all
Thy presence and thy portals, while I lay,   **portals** *gates.*
Mouth, forehead, eyelids, growing dewy-warm
With kisses balmier than half-opening buds   **balmier** *sweeter smelling,*
Of April, and could hear the lips that kiss'd   60 *more healing.*
Whispering I knew not what of wild and sweet,
Like that strange song I heard Apollo sing,   **Apollo** *god of music.*
While Ilion like a mist rose into towers.   **Ilion** *Troy.*

    Yet hold me not for ever in thine East:
How can my nature longer mix with thine?   65
Coldly thy rosy shadows bathe me, cold
Are all thy lights, and cold my wrinkled feet
Upon thy glimmering thresholds, when the steam   **thresholds** *doorways.*
Floats up from those dim fields about the homes
Of happy men that have the power to die,   70
And grassy barrows of the happier dead.   **barrows** *burial mounds.*
Release me, and restore me to the ground;
Thou seest all things, thou wilt see my grave:

156

Thou wilt renew thy beauty morn by morn;
I earth in earth forget these empty courts,   75
And thee returning on thy silver wheels.

☆

Thinking/Talking Points

▷ Why do you think Tithonus asked for immortality?
  What did he forget to ask for?

▷ What process(es) is the speaker witnessing and describing in the first four
  lines?
  Why do you think he dwells on these scenes?

▷ Which words and phrases in the poem capture Tithonus's suffering most
  vividly for you?

▷ Look again at lines 32–45 and 53–63.
  Can you work out to whom or to what Tithonus is speaking?
  Which phrases give us clues?
  Do you think his companion's presence makes Tithonus's suffering worse?

▷ Look again at lines 28–31.
  What has Tithonus realised as a result of his sufferings?

▷ What do you think Tithonus means when he talks of
  '. . . happy men that have the power to die,
  And grassy barrows of the happier dead'?

▷ How would you describe the prevailing mood of the poem?
  What are your feelings for Tithonus?

  Reread the poem carefully to see what else deserves attention before you
  choose your assignment.

Assignments

English

○ *Your Wish is my Command*
  Write a poem or short story, in the first person, about someone whose fantasy
  becomes an unexpectedly painful reality. (e.g. You might write a variation on
  the theme of Midas who asked for everything he touched to be turned to gold;
  or about somebody who marries the most attractive but not the most reliable
  person in the world; how knowledge leads to misery, or about the unpleasant
  side-effects of fame or political power. Or you may simply replicate Tithonus's
  mistake.)

English Literature

○ Essay: Write an appreciation of the way Tennyson evokes the beauty of dawn
  and dramatises the sufferings of Tithonus in this poem.
  Remember to refer closely to the text in your essay.

★

DO NOT GO GENTLE
INTO THAT GOOD NIGHT

The following poem was written as the poet's father lay dying.
Before you read it, consider what very different feelings might be running
through a young man's head in such a situation.

Do Not Go Gentle Into That Good Night

Do not go gentle into that good night,
Old age should burn and rave at close of day;
Rage, rage against the dying of the light.

Though wise men at their end know dark is right,
Because their words had forked no lightning they   5
Do not go gentle into that good night.

Good men, the last wave by, crying how bright
Their frail deeds might have danced in a green bay,
Rage, rage against the dying of the light.

Wild men who caught and sang the sun in flight,   10
And learn, too late, they grieved it on its way,
Do not go gentle into that good night.

Grave men, near death, who see with blinding sight
Blind eyes could blaze like meteors and be gay,
Rage, rage against the dying of the light.   15

And you, my father, there on the sad height,
Curse, bless, me now with your fierce tears, I pray.
Do not go gentle into that good night.
Rage, rage against the dying of the light.

☆

Thinking/Talking Points

▷ How would you describe the speaker's mood here?

▷ Can you think of two or more meanings which the word 'gentle' might have in the poem?

▷ Whose emotions do you think the speaker is describing when he urges his father to 'Rage, rage against the dying of the light'?
Why 'rage'?

▷ Why might even 'wise men' wish to postpone death?

▷ And what might 'good men' most regret as they faced it?

▷ How did the wild men hasten to their end?

▷ And what do you think is passing through the minds of 'grave men' as they face their final moments on earth?

▷ Why do you think the speaker begs his father to 'Curse, bless, me now' in the last stanza?

▷ What poetic device helps to sustain and intensify the feelings poured out in the poem?

Read the poem again now before you choose an assignment.

Assignments

English

○ *A Farewell*
See if you can put yourself into the position of someone approaching their death.
How do you think they would feel about the people, the places, the experiences they will be leaving?
What might they feel about the process of death itself?
Can you imagine somebody accepting, even welcoming death?

English Literature

○ Essay: How successfully has the poet shared the experience of losing his father?
Describe his mixture of emotions.
Do you find it a moving poem?
Remember to refer to the text in your answer.

★

BAVARIAN GENTIANS

Pluto is the God of the Underworld. He fell in love with Persephone, daughter of Demeter (the goddess of harvests), and stole her away to be his bride in the dark kingdom. Demeter searched the world for her lost daughter, neglecting the cultivation of the earth and thus bringing about the first Winter. She pleaded with Pluto to restore her daughter. Finally it was agreed that Persephone should spend half the year in the Underworld, half in this. When Persephone is with her mother, the earth is fruitful. When she returns to the Underworld, it is Winter.

In this poem, written shortly before he died, Lawrence contemplates what must come to us all.

Bavarian Gentians

Not every man has gentians in his house
in soft September, at slow, sad Michaelmas.
Bavarian gentians, tall and dark, but dark
darkening the daytime, torch-like with the smoking blueness of
                                          Pluto's gloom,
ribbed hellish flowers erect, with their blaze of darkness spread
                                          blue,   5
blown flat into points, by the heavy white draught of the day.
Torch-flowers of the blue-smoking darkness, Pluto's dark-blue blaze,
black lamps from the halls of Dis, smoking dark blue,
giving off darkness, blue darkness, upon Demeter's yellow-pale day
who have you come for, here in the white-cast day?   10
Reach me a gentian, give me a torch!
let me guide myself with the blue, forked torch of a flower
down the darker and darker stairs, where blue is darkened on
                                         bluenesss
down the way Persephone goes, just now, in first-frosted September
to the sightless realm where darkness is married to dark   15
and Persephone herself is but a voice, as a bride,
a gloom invisible enfolded in the deeper dark
of the arms of Pluto as he ravishes her once again
and pierces her once more with his passion of the utter dark
among the splendour of black-blue torches, shedding
                           fathomless darkness on the nuptials.   20

Give me a flower on a tall stem, and three dark flames,
for I will go to the wedding, and be wedding-guest
at the marriage of the living dark.

☆

Thinking/Talking Points

▷ What does the first statement in the poem suggest to you about the speaker's attitude to his approaching death?
How would you describe the mood of the poem as a whole?

▷ What images and feelings does this phrase stir in you: 'soft September, at slow, sad Michaelmas'?
Do you think Autumn is the appropriate season for the thoughts explored in the poem? Can you explain why?

▷ do you imagine when Lawrence talks of the flowers' 'blaze of darkness'?
What kind of torch are they for him?

▷ What is the answer to 'who have you come for, here in the white-cast day'?
How does the speaker respond to the summons?

▷ Look again at lines 17–21.
How would you describe the various qualities of the darkness?

▷ Describe in your own words the mood of the final lines.

Reread the poem now to see what else makes it powerful.
What pace, tempo and tone of voice would you aim for if you were reading *Bavarian Gentians* aloud?

Assignments

English

○ Has there been a painful separation of any kind in your life (e.g. losing somebody or something you loved or leaving someone or somewhere very dear to you?)
See if you can recapture that parting, in verse or in prose.

English Literature

○ Essay: Write an appreciation of *Bavarian Gentians*.
Lawrence wrote once that what he respected animals for was their utter lack of self-pity.
Do you think Lawrence manages to escape feeling sorry for himself in this?
Has the poem changed the way you feel about Death in any way?

Further reading

Lawrence   *The Ship of Death*

★

= Shakespeare =
SONNET 60

How do you imagine the *movement* of Time?

Imagine a speeded-up film of someone's life, from the cradle to the grave: think of the shapes, the gestures, the expressions on the changing face.

Sonnet 60

Like as the waves make towards the pebbled shore,
So do our minutes hasten to their end;
Each changing place with that which goes before,
In sequent toil all forwards do contend.
Nativity, once in the main of light,
Crawls to maturity, wherewith being crown'd,
Crooked eclipses 'gainst his glory fight,
And Time, that gave, doth now his gift confound.
Time doth transfix the flourish set on youth,
And delves the parallels in beauty's brow,
Feeds on the rarities of nature's truth,
And nothing stands but for his scythe to mow:
   And yet to times in hope my verse shall stand,
   Praising thy worth, despite his cruel hand.

in sequent toil one after another.
contend press forward.
nativity the newborn baby.
the main of light vigorous sunshine.
crooked malicious.
transfix shoot its arrow through.
flourish beauty, confidence.
delves digs.
parallels furrows, wrinkles.
brow forehead.
mow cut down.
in hope to come.

Assignments

○ Draw a series of pictures to illustrate one or all of the types of change Shakespeare describes.

○ Imagine a tree, a building, a landscape or a hamlet/village/town/city . . .
over a long period of time, as it grows and then decays.
Write a poem, or a series of descriptive paragraphs, or draw a series of drawings to record the process of Change.

★

= Morgan =
MESSAGE CLEAR

We suggest that you work on this assignment in small groups.

Prepare a performance of this poem.

Message Clear

```
        am                    i                              if
i   am                                              he
            he    r         o
            h         ur    t
            the    re                  and           .
            he      re               ånd
            he    re
            a                          n         d
            th    e   r                              e
i   am                 r                                     ife
                            i  n
                    s      ion   and
i                                     d          i  e
        am      e   res    ect
        am      e   res    ection
                                o                           f
            the                                     life
                        o                                   f
        m     e                 n
                    sur e
            the                         d          i  e
i                   s
                    s      e   t        and
i   am  the         sur             d
        a     t     res         t
                                o                   life
i   am  he    r                                     e
i   a                       ct
i                   r   u        n
i       m   e   e       t
i                           t                       i  e
i                   s      t         and
i   am  th              o            th
i   am              r                a
i   am  the     su          n
i   am  the     s           on
i   am  the     e   rect on             e   if
i   am              re          n           t
i   am              s               a           fe
i   am              s      e    n            t
i           he      e               d
i           t   e       t
i                   re          a   d
        a   th      re          a   d
        a           s       t on                    e
        a   t       re          a   d
        a   th      r       on                      e
i                   resurrect
                                    a               life
i   am                      i   n                   life
i   am          resurrection
i   am  the     resurrection     and
i   am
i   am  the     resurrection     and   the   life
```

★

APPENDICES

You're by Sylvia Plath

The answer to the riddle on page 10:
You're [. . . my unborn child]

Appendix 1

Eliot: *Prelude I*

Assignments 2–3

These are the words deleted from the three poems (not in the same order here as they occur in the poems):
five; coffee; beer; steaks; smell; smells; sawdust-; smoky; burnt-out; blackened; withered; broken; muddy; dingy; grimy; newspapers; block; furnished; vacant; lonely; consciousness; press; impatient; stuffing; insistent; square; assured; certain; assume; masquerades; soul.

Appendix 2

Here is the text of Eliot's *Prelude III*.

III

You tossed a blanket from the bed,
You lay upon your back, and waited;
You dozed, and watched the night revealing
The thousand sordid images
Of which your soul was constituted;   5
They flickered against the ceiling.
And when all the world came back
And the light crept up between the shutters,
And you heard the sparrows in the gutters,
You had a vision of the street   10
As the street hardly understands;
Sitting along the bed's edge, where
You curled the papers from your hair,
Or clasped the yellow soles of feet
In the palms of both soiled hands.

Appendix 3

Prelude IV
These are the seven concluding lines of the sequence:

I am moved by fancies that are curled   *10*
Around these images, and cling:
The notion of some infinitely gentle
Infinitely suffering thing.

Wipe your hand across your mouth, and laugh;
The worlds revolve like ancient women   *15*
Gathering fuel in vacant lots.

Appendix 4

Illustrations/Photographs

Acknowledgements

The following copyright poems are reprinted by permission of the copyright holders to whom grateful acknowledgement is made.

'You're', 'Spinster', 'Wuthering Heights' and 'Tulips' reprinted from *Sylvia Plath Collected Poems*, published by Faber and Faber Ltd, copyright Ted Hughes 1967, 1971, 1965 and 1981, by permission of Olwen Hughes. 'Dry August Burned' by Walter de la Mare, reproduced courtesy of the literary trustees of Walter de la Mare, and the Society of Authors as their representative. 'The Early Purges' and 'Death of a Naturalist' reprinted by permission of Faber and Faber Ltd from *Death of a Naturalist* by Seamus Heaney. 'Out, Out –' reprinted from *The Poetry of Robert Frost* edited by Edward Connery Lathem by permission of Jonathan Cape Ltd. 'The Fair' by Vernon Scannell, reprinted by permission of the author. 'Fern Hill' and 'Do Not Go Gentle Into That Good Night' by Dylan Thomas from *The Poems* (Dent). 'The Jaguar' and 'The Thought-Fox' reprinted by permission of Faber and Faber Ltd from *Hawk in the Rain* by Ted Hughes. 'Second Glance at a Jaguar' reprinted by permission of Faber and Faber Ltd from *Wodwo* by Ted Hughes. 'Rain' reprinted by permission of Faber and Faber Ltd from *Moortown* by Ted Hughes. 'Love Is . . .' and 'Without You' from *Adrian Henri Collected Poems* copyright © 1986 by Adrian Henri, used by permission. 'The Seduction' by Eileen McAuley, reprinted by permission of the author. 'The Fly' and 'Fairy Tale' from *Selected Poems* by Miroslav Holub, translated by Ian Milner and George Theiner (Penguin Modern European Poets, 1967) copyright © Miroslav Holub 1967, translations copyright © Penguin Books 1967. 'The Companion' and 'Lies' from *Selected Poems* by Yevgeny Yevtushenko, translated with an introduction by Robin Milner-Gulland and Peter Levi, S.J. (*Penguin Modern European Poets*, 1962) copyright © Robin Milner-Gulland and Peter Levi, 1962. 'More Light! More Light!' reprinted from *The Hard Hours* by Anthony Hecht (1979) by permission of Oxford University Press. 'The Horses' reprinted by permission of Faber and Faber Ltd from *The Collected Poems* of Edwin Muir. 'Why Patriots are a Bit Nuts in the Head' by Roger McGough from *Penguin Modern Poets 10*, reprinted by permission of A.D. Peters & Co. Ltd. 'Hot Night on Water Street' copyright © 1957 by Louis Simpson reprinted from *A Dream of Governors* by permission of Wesleyan University Press. 'After Midnight' © Louis Simpson 1966, reprinted from Louis Simpson's *Selected Poems* (1966) by permission of Oxford University Press. 'A Polished Performance' reprinted from *Collected Poems* (1981) by D.J. Enright, courtesy of Watson, Little Ltd. 'The Produce District' reprinted by permission of Faber and Faber Ltd from *Touch* by Thom Gunn. 'Preludes' and 'The Love Song of J. Alfred Prufrock' reprinted by permission of Faber and Faber Ltd from *Collected Poems 1909–1962* by T.S. Eliot. 'The Unknown Citizen' reprinted by permission of Faber and Faber Ltd from *Collected Poems* by W.H. Auden. 'Au Jardin des Plantes' © John Wain 1961, reproduced by permission of Curtis Brown, London. 'On the Move' reprinted by permission of Faber and Faber Ltd from *The Sense of Movement* by Thom Gunn. The extract from *Shakespeare Made Easy: Macbeth* by Alan Durband reprinted by permission of Century Hutchinson Ltd. 'Hawk Roosting' reprinted by permission of Faber and Faber Ltd from *Lupercal* by Ted Hughes. 'Message Clear' reprinted by permission of Carcanet Press Ltd from *Poems of Thirty Years* (1982) by Edwin Morgan.

Every effort has been made to reach copyright holders; the publishers would be glad to hear from anyone whose rights they have unknowingly infringed.

Thanks are due to the following for permission to reproduce photographs:

p. 7 Elliot Erwitt/Magnum, and The John Hillelson Agency Ltd; p. 40 Eddy Posthuma de Boer; pp. 47, 104 Ad van Denderen; pp. 55, 155 Windsor Royal Library, © Her Majesty the Queen; p. 67 The Trustees of the Imperial War Museum; p. 76 Griffiths/Magnum, and the John Hillelson Agency Ltd; p. 89 Cambridge Evening News; p. 85 Colorific © TIME inc.